SpringerBriefs in Computer Science

Series Editors
Stan Zdonik
Peng Ning
Shashi Shekhar
Jonathan Katz
Xindong Wu
Lakhmi C Jain
David Padua
Xuemin Shen
Borko Furht

For further volumes:
http://www.springer.com/series/10028

K. K. Shukla · M. V. Prasad

Lossy Image Compression

Domain Decomposition-Based Algorithms

 Springer

Prof. K. K. Shukla
Department of Computer Engineering
Indian Institute of Technology
Banaras Hindu University
Varanasi 221005
India
e-mail: kkshukla.cse@itbhu.ac.in

Asst. Prof. M. V. Prasad
Institute for Development and Research
  in Banking Technology
Castle Hills, Road No. 1
Hyderabad 500057
India
e-mail: mvnkprasad@idrbt.ac.in

ISSN 2191-5768
ISBN 978-1-4471-2217-3
DOI 10.1007/978-1-4471-2218-0
Springer London Dordrecht Heidelberg New York

e-ISSN 2191-5776
e-ISBN 978-1-4471-2218-0

British Library Cataloguing in Publication Data
A catalogue record for this book is available from the British Library

Cover design: eStudio Calamar, Berlin/Figueres

Printed on acid-free paper

Springer is part of Springer Science+Business Media (www.springer.com)

Preface

Image data compression is concerned with minimization of the number of information carrying units used to represent an image. Image compression schemes can be divided into two broad classes: lossless compression schemes and lossy compression schemes. Lossless compression techniques, as their name implies aim at exact reconstruction and involve no loss of information. Lossy compression techniques accept some loss of information, therefore images compressed using a lossy technique cannot be reconstructed exactly. The distortion in the image caused by lossy compression may be imperceptible to humans and we obtain much higher compression ratios than is possible with lossless compression. Lossy compression scheme can be further divided into three major categories: 1. Transform coding, 2. Fractal image compression, and 3. Domain Decomposition. Joint Photographic Expert Group (JPEG), JPEG2000, Binary Tree Triangular Coding (BTTC) etc. are the examples of lossy image compression methods. This book describes five new domain decomposition based lossy image compression algorithms, evaluation of their performance and their parallel implementation.

Organization of the book is as follows. Chapter 1 brings the subject matter into perspective and presents a historical review of image compression in moderate detail. Chapter 2 presents four new image compression algorithms namely, Three-triangle decomposition scheme, Six-triangle decomposition scheme, Nine-triangle decomposition scheme and 4. Delaunay Triangulation Scheme. Performance of these algorithms is evaluated using standard test images. The asymptotic time complexity of Three-, Six-, and Nine-triangle decomposition algorithms is the same: $O(nlogn)$ for coding and $\theta(n)$ for decoding. The time complexity of the Delaunay triangulation algorithm is $O(n^2logn)$ for coding and $O(nlogn)$ for decoding, where n is the number of pixels in the image.

Chapter 3 presents more domain decomposition algorithms using quality measures like Average Difference (AD), Entropy (H), Mean Squared Error (MSE) and a fuzzy geometry measure called Fuzzy Compactness (FC). All the partitioning methods discussed in this chapter execute in $O(nlogn)$ time for encoding and $\theta(n)$ time for decoding, where n is the number of pixels in the image.

Chapter 4 presents parallel version of domain decomposition algorithms on different architectures like Concurrent Read Exclusive Write (CREW) Parallel Random Access Machine (PRAM), Hypercube, 2-D Mesh, and Sparse Mesh. Time complexities of these algorithms are also derived. Implementation of the domain decomposition algorithm on Parallel Virtual Machine (PVM) environment using Master-Slave paradigm has been described. Parallel program profiles and speed up measurements are given.

Finally, concluding remarks and future research directions are discussed Chap. 5.

A comprehensive bibliography related to the field is included at the end.

Prof. K. K. Shukla
Asst. Prof. M. V. Prasad

Contents

1	**Introduction**	1
	1.1 Importance of Image Compression.	1
	1.2 Classification of Image Compression Techniques	2
	1.2.1 Lossless Image Compression	2
	1.2.2 Lossy Image Compression	3
	1.3 JPEG Standard	3
	1.4 JPEG 2000 Standard	3
	1.5 Historical Review	4
	1.6 Major Contributions of the Book.	5
	References	9

2	**Tree Triangular Coding Image Compression Algorithms**.	13
	2.1 Background Material	14
	2.2 Introduction	15
	2.3 Coding Scheme.	17
	2.3.1 Binary Tree Triangular Coding (BTTC) Scheme.	18
	2.3.2 Three Triangle Decomposition Scheme	20
	2.3.3 Interpolation Error.	23
	2.3.4 Six Triangle Decomposition Scheme	26
	2.3.5 Nine Triangle Decomposition Scheme.	28
	2.3.6 Delaunay Triangulation Scheme	31
	2.4 Experimental Results.	34
	2.5 Conclusions	38
	References	40

3	**Image Compression Using Quality Measures**.	43
	3.1 Space Decomposition.	43
	3.1.1 Image Quality Measures	45
	3.1.2 Fuzzy Geometric Measures	45

3.2   Coding Scheme   47
      3.2.1   Average Difference   48
      3.2.2   Entropy   48
      3.2.3   Normalized Mean Square Error   48
      3.2.4   Fuzzy Compactness   49
      3.2.5   Computing Time   51
3.3   Experimental Results   51
3.4   Conclusions   57
References   63

4 Parallel Image Compression Algorithms   65
4.1   Parallel Domain Decomposition   65
4.2   Coding Scheme   67
      4.2.1   Implementation on CREW PRAM Model   67
      4.2.2   Implementation on Hypercube Model   70
      4.2.3   Implementation on 2D Mesh Model   72
      4.2.4   Implementation on Sparse Mesh   74
      4.2.5   Implementation on PVM   76
4.3   Experimental Results   81
4.4   Conclusions   85
References   86

5 Conclusions and Future Directions   87
5.1   Concluding Remarks   87
5.2   Future Directions   89

Symbols and Notations

A	Signed area of triangle
l_i	Edge length of a triangle
α_i	Signed altitudes of a triangle
r_i	Signed radius of an element
θ_i	Angle at vertex v_i of triangle
N_n	Number of nodes in triangular mesh
E_n	Number of edges in triangular mesh
T_n	Number of triangles in triangular mesh
$F(.)$	Original gray value of the image
$F'(.)$	Gray value of the reconstructed image
$G(.)$	Predicted gray value of the image using linear interpolation
L	List of leaves
M	Image size
H	Height of fuzzy set
W	Width of fuzzy set
L	Length of fuzzy set
B	Breadth of fuzzy set
A	Area of fuzzy set
P	Number of processors
$O(.)$	Asymptotic upper bound
$\Omega(.)$	Asymptotic lower bound
$\Theta(.)$	Asymptotic upper and lower bound

Abbreviations

AD	Average difference
BAS	Binary adaptive segmentation
BSP	Binary space partitioning
BTTC	Binary tree triangular coding
CQ	Correlation quality
CR	Compression ratio
CREW	Concurrent read and exclusive write
DCT	Discrete cosine transform
DFT	Discrete fourier transform
DWT	Discrete wavelet transform
FC	Fuzzy compactness
H	Entropy
ICT	Irreversible component transform
IF	Image fidelity
IOAC	Index of area coverage
JPEG	Joint photographic expert group
JPEG 2000	Joint photographic expert group 2000
LMSE	Laplacian mean square error
MD	Maximum difference
MSE	Mean square error
NAE	Normalized absolute error
NK	Normalized cross-correlation
NMSE	Normalized mean square error
PMSE	Peak mean square error
PRAM	Parallel random access machine
PSNR	Peak signal to noise ratio

PVM	Parallel virtual machine
RCT	Reversible component transform
SC	Structural content
SIC	Segmentation based image coding
SIMD	Single instruction multiple data
SPMD	Single program multiple data
WD	Weighted distance

Chapter 1
Introduction

Abstract This chapter brings the subject matter into perspective and presents a historical review of image compression in moderate detail.

Keywords Image compression · JPEG · BTTC · Domain decomposition

Image data compression is concerned with coding of data to minimize the number of bits used to represent an image. Sampling of a band-limited image is a straightforward approach to data compression, where an infinite number of image points per unit sampling area are reduced to a single image sample. In digital image processing, each image sample called a *pixel* or *pel*, is quantized to a sufficient number of bits before the image is stored (or transmitted) digitally. Data compression is useful in storage and transmission of images [1–4]. The aim is to minimize the memory for storage and bandwidth for transmission of digital images. A compressed image, when decoded to reconstruct its original form may be accompanied by some distortion. The efficiency of a compression algorithm is measured by its data compressing ability, the resulting distortion and its implementation complexity. The complexity of data compression algorithms is also an important consideration in their hardware implementation.

1.1 Importance of Image Compression

A 500 × 500 color image, with uncompressed format of 24 bits/pixel (bpp) will require about 100 s. of transmission time over a 64 Kbps link. With 0.25 bpp compression coding the transmission time is reduced to about 1 s. Typical television images have spatial resolution of approximately 512 × 512 pels/frame. At 8-bit/pel intensity resolution and 30 frames/s this translates into a rate of nearly

K. K. Shukla and M. V. Prasad, *Lossy Image Compression*,
SpringerBriefs in Computer Science, DOI: 10.1007/978-1-4471-2218-0_1,
© K. K. Shukla 2011

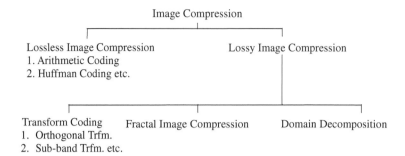

Fig. 1.1 Image compression classification tree

60×10^6 bit/s. Depending on the application, digital image raw data rates typically vary from 10^5 bit/frame to 10^8 bit/frame or 10^6 bit/s to 10^9 bit/s or higher.

On a Compact Disk (CD) 20 kHz audio is sampled at 44.1 kHz and stored at 16 bit/sample, 8,706 Kbps/sound channel. Various audio compression algorithms provide CD quality sound at 128 Kbps/channel. Image compression capabilities are also central to applications that combine audio and visual functions such as CD-ROM multimedia and digital television with multiple sound channels.

It is thus clear that image compression is a crucial technology for a large set of multimedia based applications that depend upon space efficient storage and transmission of images over a limited bandwidth.

1.2 Classification of Image Compression Techniques

Image data compression schemes can be divided into two broad classes: *lossless compression scheme* and *lossy compression scheme* [5, 6]. The image compression methods classification tree is shown in Fig. 1.1.

1.2.1 Lossless Image Compression

Lossless compression techniques, as their name implies, involve no loss of information during coding. If data have undergone lossless compression, the original data can be recovered exactly from the compressed data. Lossless compression is generally used for discrete data, such as text, computer-generated data and some kinds of image and video information. Text compression is an important application for lossless compression. It is very important that the reconstruction is identical to the original text, as very small differences can result in statements with very different meaning. Arithmetic coding, Huffman coding etc. are the examples of lossless image data compression techniques.

1.2.2 Lossy Image Compression

Lossy compression techniques involve some loss of information, therefore data that have been compressed using lossy techniques cannot be recovered or reconstructed exactly. In return for accepting this distortion in reconstruction, we generally obtain much higher compression ratios than is possible with lossless compression. Lossy compression scheme can be further divided into three major categories: (1) Transform coding, (2) Fractal image compression, and (3) Domain decomposition.

Joint Photographic Expert Group (JPEG), JPEG2000, Binary Tree Triangular Coding (BTTC) [7] etc. are the examples of lossy image compression method. This book describes various newly proposed domain decomposition based lossy image compression algorithms.

1.3 JPEG Standard

The goal of JPEG is to provide continuous-tone image compression, which meets the following requirements [8–14] (www.npac.syr/edu/education/pub/demos/paralleljpeg.html):

1. Be at or near the state of the art with regard to compression rate and accompanying image fidelity.
2. Be applicable to practically any kind of continuous-tone digital source image
3. Have tractable computational complexity
4. Have the following modes of operation:

   - Sequential encoding,
   - Progressive encoding,
   - Lossless encoding, and
   - Hierarchical encoding

   It is based on the discrete cosine transform.

1.4 JPEG 2000 Standard

The JPEG 2000 standard provides a set of features that are of importance to many high-end emerging applications. Some of the most important features that this standard provides are the following [15–20]:

- Superior low bit-rate performance,
- Lossless and lossy compression,
- Progressive transmission,

- Region-of-interest coding,
- Random code stream access/processing,
- Robustness to bit-errors,
- Open architecture,
- Content-based description,
- Side channel spatial information,
- Protective image security, and
- Continuous-tone and bi-level compression.

It is based on the discrete wavelet transform.

These standard methods form the basis of comparison for the new algorithms discussed in this book.

Readers interested in details of these standards can find them in the references listed.

1.5 Historical Review

Jain [21] has described a large variety of algorithms for image data compression. The algorithms discussed can be easily adopted to multi dimensional data compression. Linde et al. [22] gave an efficient algorithm for the design of vector quantizer that is based either on a known probabilistic model or on a long training sequence of data. Rosenfeld [23] defined intrinsic and extrinsic diameter for fuzzy subsets, which reduce to the ordinary definitions when subsets are crisp and also defined height and width for a fuzzy subset. Rosenfeld [24] defined perimeter for fuzzy subsets of the plane and showed that it reduces to standard definition if the fuzzy set is an ordinary subset. Pal et al. [25] reported algorithms based on minimization of compactness of fuzziness. Pal et al. [26] proposed some useful geometric properties *viz.* length, breadth, index of area coverage (IOAC) of a fuzzy set along with their computational aspects.

Wallance [10] described the implementation issues of JPEG. Pal et al. [27] attempted to demonstrate a way of implementing the concept of fuzzy geometry in image processing/analysis problems. Some new measures were proposed *viz.* density, adjacency and center of gravity. Pal et al. [28] gave a review of segmentation techniques. They discussed both fuzzy and non-fuzzy techniques including color image segmentation and neural network based approaches. Interpolation of fuzzy data by a continuous fuzzy valued function and numerical methods for calculating the fuzzy interpolant were given by Kaleva [29].

Eskicioglu et al. [30] evaluated a number of quality measures for gray scale image compression. They use bivariate models, exploiting the differences between corresponding pixels in the original and degraded images. Fuzzy vector quantization algorithms were developed and evaluated by Karayiannis et al. [31]. A tree structured segmentation framework of a predictive multi-resolution image coder exploiting the statistical dependency between the layers of the image pyramid was proposed by Wu et al. [32]. Bramble [33] presented a finite element procedure consisting of finding an appropriate solution in the form of piecewise linear functions or piecewise quadratic etc. Most frequently used approaches triangulate the domain such that the internal angles of every triangle should not be too small. Babuska et al. [34] have shown that the minimum angle condition is not essential but no angle should be close to 180°. Rippa [35] concluded that triangles should be long in a direction where the magnitude of second order directional derivative of function F is small and thin in direction where the magnitude of the second directional derivative of F is large for a good piecewise linear interpolation of surface using triangulation.

Aurenhammer et al. [36] reported triangulating a convex polygon using n Steiner points under the following optimality criteria: (1) minimizing the overall edge length ratio; (2) minimizing the maximum edge length; and (3) minimizing the maximum triangle perimeter. Their algorithm runs in $O(n^2 \log n)$ time using $O(n)$ space. Diwan et al. [37] proved that plane triangulations are six-partitionable. Mitra et al. [38] proposed image magnification using the theory of fractals. Eckert et al. [39] identified how various perceptual components have been incorporated in their quality metrics, and identified a number of psycho-physical testing techniques that can be used to validate the metrics. Sadeh [40] studied a transform method for compressing digital data on a two dimensional lattice based on polynomial approximation and found the properties of set of matrix compressors that minimize the distance, the matrix transform and the error. Significant research on image compression is summarized in Table 1.1.

1.6 Major Contributions of the Book

- Four new fast image compression algorithms and implementation of these algorithms are presented. It is shown that quality of the reconstructed image using new algorithms is almost equal to JPEG.
- A detailed study of fuzzy geometry measures and their application to image compression algorithms is given.
- New domain decomposition algorithms using image quality measures are presented. Various quality measures for gray scale image compression are discussed.
- Domain decomposition algorithms on different parallel architectures are described and evaluation of time complexity of parallel algorithms is given.
- Implementation of decomposition algorithms on a cluster of distributed computing system in Parallel Virtual Machine (PVM) environment is discussed and PVM program execution profile and speedup are given.

In the next chapter, we describe the basic BTTC algorithm and its new improved variants. Computational complexity analysis and comparative test results of the new algorithms are also presented.

Table 1.1 Summary of research on image compression and related topics

Reference no	Year of publication	Authors name	Remarks
[41]	2003	Prasad et al.	Proposed space decomposition algorithms using quality measures *viz.* Average difference (AD), Entropy (H), Mean Squared Error (MSE) and Fuzzy Compactness (FC). FC gave better quality compared to remaining algorithms proposed
[42]	2003	Biswas	The compression algorithm encodes a gray level image through global approximations of sub-images by 2D- Bezier—Bernstein polynomial along with corrections, if needed. Contours are approximated by 1D Bezier—Bernstein polynomial and texture, if present, by Huffman coding scheme using Hilbert scan on texture blocks. Order of the 2D polynomials has been computed with the help of an image quality index (IQI).The proposed compression algorithm examines the compression result by encoding contours through their approximation based on stretching of discrete circular arcs. Stretching is done by affine transformations
[43]	2003	Cheng et al.	Fuzzy homogeneity and scale space approach to color image segmentation is proposed. The fuzzy homogeneity histogram is employed. Both global and local information are considered when we process fuzzy homogeneity histogram. The scale space filter is utilized for analyzing fuzzy homogeneity histogram to find appropriate segments of the homogeneity histogram bounded by local extrema of derivatives
[44]	2003	Redford	Describes speeding up JPEG on an eight-way parallel vector DSP
[45]	2002	Prasad et al.	BTTC image compression algorithm has been implemented using a fuzzy technique. It gives better noise immunity compared to BTTC
[46]	2002	Prasad et al.	Parallel implementation of segmented algorithm has been proposed on a cluster of distributed computing system in Parallel Virtual Machine (PVM) environment in order to obtain speedup
[47]	2002	Plaza et al.	Proved that sequence of meshes constructed by applying a skeleton regular partition over each element of the preceding mesh have an associated set of difference equations which relate the number of elements, faces, edges and vertices of the nth and (n−1)th meshes
[48]	2002	Boissonnat et al.	Describes an algorithm to reconstruct smooth surfaces of arbitrary topology from unorganized sample points and normals. The method uses natural neighbor interpolation and accommodates non-uniform samples. The reconstructed surface interpolates the data points and is implicitly represented as the zero set of some pseudo distance function
[49]	2001	Prasad et al.	Presented a new three triangle domain decomposition image compression algorithm. These algorithms execute in $O(nlogn)$ for encoding and $\theta(n)$ for decoding, where n is the number of image pixels
[50]	2001	Lundmark et al.	For hexagonally sampled images hierarchical sub-sampling structure is given which yields hexagon like regions with fractal borders

(continued)

Table 1.1 (continued)

Reference no	Year of publication	Authors name	Remarks
[51]	2001	Vreelj et al.	Direct B-Spline filter can safely be replaced with a short FIR filter without compromising performance
[52]	2001	Fan et al.	A hybrid image segmentation technique has been proposed by integrating the results of color extraction and SRG, in which the centroids between the obtained edge regions are used as the initial seeds for the SRG procedure
[53]	2001	Kotlov	Authors derive the tree width and regular triangulation for a spectral graph invariant
[54]	2000	Miguet et al.	Introduced two fully parallel heuristics that compute the suboptimal partitioning with better complexity than best known algorithms and compared the two heuristics to an optimal partitioning both in terms of execution time and accuracy of partition
[55]	2000	Sibeyn	A sparse mesh, which has processing units (PUs) on the diagonal grid only, is a cost effective distributed memory machine. Various fundamental problems are analyzed proving that sparse meshes have great potential
[56]	2000	Rosenfeld	Author presents a bibliography of computer vision and image analysis. The topics covered include computational techniques; feature detection and segmentation; image and scene analysis; etc. References are also given on related topics, including geometry and graphics, compression and processing, sensors and optics, visual perception, neural networks, artificial intelligence and pattern recognition, as well as on applications
[17]	2000	Chistopoulos et al.	JPEG2000 is being designed to address the requirement of diversity of applications, e.g., Internet, color facsimile, printing, scanning, medical imagery etc.
[57]	2000	Weinberger et al.	LOCO-I (Low complexity lossless compression for images) is based on simple fixed context model, which approaches the capability of the more complex universal techniques for capturing high-order dependencies. LOCO-I attains compression ratios similar or superior to those obtained with state-of-the-art schemes
[58]	2000	Taubman	EBCOT algorithm exhibits state-of-the-art compression performance, producing a bit stream with rich set of features including resolution, SNR and scalability together with random access property. It is suitable for applications involving remote browsing of large compressed images
[59]	2000	de Queiroz et al.	Presented block thresholding to segment an image for mixed raster content and optimized the block threshold in a rate-distortion sense
[60]	1999	Wang et al.	Described method to adaptively adjust in three dimensions, triangular plane patches that approximate the corresponding luminance curved surface of an original image. Such an adjustment considers the influence of all pixels contained in the projection patch

(continued)

Table 1.1 (continued)

Reference no	Year of publication	Authors name	Remarks
[61]	1999	Toivanen et al.	Proposed new image compression method based on the distance transform on curved surface (DTOCS) which calculates an integer approximation of weighted pseudo- Euclidean distance transform along discrete eight- paths
[62]	1998	Miyahara et al.	A new methodology presented for the determination of objective metric for still image coding is reported. This methodology is applied to obtain a picture quality scale (PQS) for the coding of chromatic images over full rage image quality. PQS takes into account the properties of visual perception for both global features and localized disturbances
[63]	1998	Rosenfeld	Brief review work on the fuzzy topology and geometry of image subsets, including adjacency, separation and connectedness; distance and relative position; area, perimeter and diameter; convexity; medial axes and thinning; as well as applications of these concepts in image processing and analysis
[64]	1997	Mitchell	Showed that straight-line graph or polygon with holes covering triangulation has minimum angle at least a constant factor times upper bound
[10]	1997	Distasi et al.	Described an algorithm (BTTC) based on recursive decomposition of image domain into right- angled triangles arranged in binary tree. The method is attractive because of its fast encoding $O(nlogn)$ and decoding $\theta(n)$, where n is the number of pixels
[65]	1996	Radha et al.	Came out with a new image segmentation based coding method that divides the desired image using binary space partitioning (BSP). This approach partitions the desired image recursively by arbitrarily oriented lines in a hierarchical manner
[66]	1996	Davoine et al.	Proposed a new scheme for fractal image compression based on adaptive Delaunay triangulation. The classification step is based on modified version of Llyod algorithm in order to reduce the encoding complexity

References

1. Pratt WK (1978) Digital image processing. Wiley, New York, pp 591–710
2. Pratt WK (1979) Image transmission techniques. Academic press, New York
3. AN Netravali, JO Limb (1980) Picture coding: a review. In: Proceeings of IEEE, vol 68. pp 366–406, Mar 1980
4. Special issue on bandwidth communication (1977) IEEE Transactions on communications, Nov 1977
5. Sayood K (1996) Introduction to data compression. Margan Kaufman, San Francisco
6. Nelson M, Gailly JL (1996) The data compression book, 2nd edn. M&T Publishing Inc, New York
7. Distasi R, Nappi M, Vitulano S (1997) Image compression by B-tree triangular coding. IEEE Trans Commun 45(9):1095–1100
8. Digital compression and coding of continuous-tone still images, part I, requirements and guidelines (1991) ISO/IEC JTC1 Committee draft 10918-1, Feb 1991
9. Digital compression and coding of continuous-tone still images, part II, Compliance draft (1991) ISO/IEC JTC1 Committee draft 10918-2
10. Wallace GK (1991) The JPEG still picture compression standard. Commun ACM 34:30–44
11. Gregory W, Delp J (1993) The use of high performance computing in JPEG image compression. In: Twenty seventh conference on signal, systems, and computers, Pacific Grove, California
12. Cook GW, Delp J (1994) An investigation of JPEG image and video compression using parallel processing. In: Proceedings of ICASSP, pp 437–440
13. Cook GW, Delp DJ (1996) An investigation of scalable SIMD I/O techniques with application to parallel JPEG compression. J Parallel Distrib Comput 53:111–128
14. Jiang J, Grecos C (2001) A low cost design of rate controlled JPEG-LS near lossless image compression. Image Vis Comput 19:153–164
15. Boliek M, Christopoulos C, Majani E (2000) JPEG2000 part I final draft international standard. (ISO/IEC FDIS15444-1), ISO/IES JTC/SC29/WG1n1855, Aug 2000
16. The JPEG2000 still image compression standard—ISO/IEC/JTC 1/SC 29/WG 1, Report Sep 2001
17. Christopoulos C, Skodras A, Ebrahimi T (2000) The JPEG2000 still image coding system: an overview. IEEE Trans Consum Electron 46(4):1103–1127
18. Skodras AN, Christopoulos CA, Ebrahimi T (2001) JPEG2000: the upcoming still image compression standard. Pattern Recognit Lett 22:1337–1345
19. Taubman D, Ordentlich E, Weinberger M, Seroussi G (2002) Embedded block coding in JPEG2000. Signal Process Image Commun 17:49–72
20. Askelof J, Carlander M, Christopoulos C (2002) Region of interest coding in JPEG2000. Signal Process Image Commun 17:105–111
21. AK Jain (1981) Image data compression: a review. In: Proceedings of the IEEE, vol 69, p 3
22. Linde Y, Buzo A, Gray RM (1980) An algorithm for vector quantizer design. IEEE Trans Commun 28(1):84–94
23. Rosenfeld A (1984) The diameter of fuzzy set. Fuzzy Sets Syst 13:241–246
24. Rosenfeld A, Haber S (1985) The perimeter of fuzzy set. Pattern Recognit 18:125–130
25. Pal SK, Rosenfeld A (1988) Image enhancement and thresholding by optimization of fuzzy compactness. Pattern Recognit Lett 7:77–86
26. Pal SK, Ghosh A (1990) Index of area coverage of fuzzy image subsets and extraction. Pattern Recognit Lett 831–841
27. Pal SK, Ghosh A (1992) Fuzzy geometry in image analysis. Fuzzy Sets Syst 48(1):22–40
28. Pal NR, Pal S (1993) A review on image segmentation techniques. Pattern Recognit 26:1277–1294
29. Kaleva O (1994) Interpolation of fuzzy data. Fuzzy Sets Syst 61:63–70

30. Eskicioglu AM, Fisher PS (1995) Image quality measures and their performance. IEEE Trans Commun 43(12):2959–2965
31. Karayiannis NB, Pai P-I (1995) Fuzzy vector quantization algorithms and their applications in image compression. IEEE Trans Image process 4(9):1193–1201
32. Wu Xiaolin, Fang Yonggang (1995) A segmentation-based predictive multiresolution image coder. IEEE Trans Image Process 4:34–47
33. Bramble JH, Zlamal M (1970) Triangular elements in the finite elements method. Math Comput 24(112):809–820
34. Babuska I, Aziz AK (1976) On the angle condition in the finite element method. Siam J Numer Anal 13(2):214–226
35. Rippa S (1992) Long and thin triangles can be good for linear interpolation. Siam J Numer Anal 29(1):257–270
36. Aurenhammer F, Katoh N, Kojima H, Ohsaki M, Xu Y (2002) Approximating uniform triangular meshes in polygons. Theor Comput Sci 289:879–895
37. Diwan AA, Kurhekar MP (2002) Plane triangulations are 6-partitionable. Discrete Math 256:91–103
38. Mitra SK, Murthy CA, Kundu MK (2000) A technique for image magnification using partitioned iterative function system. Pattern Recognit 33:1119–1133
39. Eckert MP, Bradley AP (1998) Perceptual quality metrics applied to still image compression. Signal Process 70:177–200
40. Sadesh I (1996) Polynomial approximation of images. Comput Math Appl 32(5):99–115
41. Prasad MVNK, Mishra VN, Shukla KK (2003) Space partitioning based image compression using quality measures. Appl Soft Comput Elsevier Sci 3:273–282
42. Biswas S (2003) Segmentation based compression for gray level images. Pattern Recognit 36:1501–1517
43. Cheng HD, Li J (2003) Fuzzy homogeneity and scale space approach to color image segmentation. Pattern Recognit 36:1545–1562
44. J Redford (2003) Parallelizing JPEG. In: ISPC proceedings, Dallas, March 21–April 3
45. Prasad MVNK, Mishra VN, Shukla KK (2002) Implementation of BTTC image compression algorithm on parallel virtual machine. J Comput Soc India 32(3):1–8, ISSN 0254-7813
46. Guibas L, Stolfi J (1985) Primitives for the manipulation of general subdivisions and the computation of voronoi diagrams. ACM Trans Graph 4(2):74–123
47. Plaza A, Rivara M-C (2002) On the adjacencies of triangular meshes based on skeleton-regular partitions. J Comput Appl Math 140:673–693
48. Boissonnant JD, Cazals F (2002) Smooth surface reconstruction via natural neighbour interpolation of distance functions. Comput Geom 22:185–203
49. Aurenhammer F (1991) Voronoi diagrams—a survey of a fundamental geometric data structure. ACM Comput Surv 23(3):345–405
50. Lundmark A, Wadstromer N, Li H (2001) Hierarchical subsampling giving fractal regions. IEEE Trans Image Process 4(1):167–173
51. Vreelj B, Vaidyanathan PP (2001) Efficient implementation of all digital interpolation. IEEE Trans Image Process 10(11):1639–1646
52. Fan J, Yau DKY, Elmagarmid AK, Araf G (2001) Automatic image segmentation by integrating color edge extraction on image processing. IEEE Trans Image Process 10(10):1454–1466
53. Kotlov A (2001) Note: tree width and regular triangulations. Discrete Math 237:187–191
54. Miguet S, Pierson JM (2000) Quality and complexity bounds of load balancing algorithms for parallel image processing. Int J Pattern Recognit Artif Intell 14(4):463–476
55. Sibeyn JF (2000) Solving fundamental problems on sparse-meshes. IEEE Trans Parallel Distrib Syst 11(12):1324–1332
56. Rosenfeld A (2000) Survey image analysis and computer vision: 1999. Comput Vis Image Underst 78:222–302

57. Weinberger MJ, Seroussi G, Sapiro G (2000) The LOCO–I lossless image compression algorithm: principles and standardization into JPEG-LS. IEEE Trans Image Process 9(8):1309–1324

58. Taubman D (2000) High performance scalable image compression with EBCOT. IEEE Trans Image Process 9(7):1158–1170

59. de Queiroz RL (2000) Optimizing block-thresholding segmentation for multilayer compression of compound images. IEEE Trans Image Process 9(9):1461–1471

60. wang L, He L, Mutoh A, Nakamura T, Itoh H (1999) Fuzzy reasoning for image compression using adaptive triangular plane patches. Fuzzy Sets Syst 113:277–284

61. Toivanen PJ, Vepsalainen AM, Parkkinen JPS (1999) Image compression using the distance transform on curved space (DTOCS) and Delaunay triangulation. Pattern Recognit Lett 20:1015–1026

62. Miyahara M, Kotani K, Algazi VR (1998) Objective picture quality scale (PQS) for image coding. IEEE Trans Image Process 46(5):1215–1225

63. Rosenfield A (1998) Fuzzy geometry: an updated overview. Inf Sci 110:123–133

64. Mitchell SA (1997) Approximating the maximum-angle covering triangulation. Comput Geom 7:93–111

65. Radha H, Vetterli M, Leonardi R (1996) Image compression using binary space partitioning trees. IEEE Trans Image Process 5(12):1610–1623

66. Davoine F, Antonini M, Chassery J-M, Barlaud M (1996) Fractal image compression based on delaunay triangulation and vector quantization. IEEE Trans Image Process 5(2):338–346

Chapter 2
Tree Triangular Coding Image Compression Algorithms

Abstract This chapter presents four new image compression algorithms namely, Three-triangle decomposition scheme, Six-triangle decomposition scheme, Nine-triangle decomposition scheme and the Delaunay Triangulation Scheme. Performance of these algorithms is evaluated using standard test images. The asymptotic time complexity of Three-, Six-, and Nine-triangle decomposition algorithms is the same: $O(nlogn)$ for coding and $\theta(n)$, for decoding. The time complexity of the Delaunay triangulation algorithm is $O(n^2logn)$ for coding and $O(nlogn)$ for decoding, where n is the number of pixels in the image.

Keywords Triangulation · Decomposition schemes · Delaunay triangulation · Algorithm complexity

This chapter presents four new image compression algorithms. Out of these, three algorithms are improvements of the recently published binary tree triangular coding (BTTC) [1]. These algorithms are based on recursive decomposition of the image domain into triangles where the new triangle vertex is located at the point of maximum prediction error and does not require the constraints of right-angled isosceles triangle and square image as in previous algorithm. These algorithms execute in $O(nlogn)$ time for encoding and $\theta(n)$ time for decoding, where n is the number of image pixels. Simulation results show that the new algorithms have a significant execution time advantage over conventional BTTC while providing quality of reconstructed image as good as BTTC. This improvement is obtained by eliminating a major weakness of the standard BTTC, where the algorithm does not utilize the point of maximum error for domain decomposition despite performing an exhaustive search (in the worst case) over the triangular domain. The fourth algorithm is based on Delaunay triangulation and executes in $O(n^2logn)$ time for encoding and $O(nlogn)$ time for decoding. The new vertex is placed at the barycenter of the triangle. The quality of the reconstructed image using Delaunay triangulation is almost equal to BTTC. This is the first time that Delaunay triangulation is applied to construct a domain decomposition based image compression algorithm.

In Sect. 2.1 domain decomposition methods are examined briefly. Definition of triangulation is given in Sect. 2.2. Section 2.3 elaborates four new algorithms and estimates their computational time complexity. Experimental results of all four algorithms on various test images are given in Sect. 2.4. Section 2.5 concludes the chapter.

2.1 Background Material

Distasi, Nappi and Vitulano [1–9] introduced the BTTC algorithm by assuming that the image to be compressed is square and that the image dimension is an integer power of 2. Their algorithm recursively decomposes the image into isosceles right angle triangles. The triangle T is divided into two triangles by splitting along its height relative to the hypotenuse. If the sub division procedure is iterated indefinitely, we eventually obtain a minimal triangle comprising of only three pixels, namely their vertices (worst case boundary condition). The relevant information is stored in a hierarchical structure namely, a binary tree. The hierarchical structure also stores the vertices gray values. In decompression, the gray values within the triangle are approximated by linear interpolation using gray values at the triangle vertices.

Although BTTC seems to perform well, its weakness is that it ignores the information about the point of maximum prediction error, which is available to the algorithm without any additional computational cost. In the following sections, we introduce three modifications to the BTTC by placing a new vertex at the point of maximum prediction error. All these algorithms result in significant reduction in depth of recursion while offering image quality comparable to BTTC.

In [10] Wu and Fang Proposed segmentation-based predictive multi-resolution image coder with time complexity $O((N_x N_y)^{1.5} log K)$ for encoding where N_x, N_y is the size of the image and K is the number of final segments (leaf nodes) in the tree. In this method, to achieve uniform progress of image reconstruction while keeping the optimal binary adaptive segmentation (BAS) tree structure, we can transmit the tree in an adaptive order. The obvious solution is to always cut the node dynamically growing BAS tree front that has the largest approximation error. Unfortunately, in this situation the decoder needs additional side information to synchronize with encoder since otherwise, it does not know which node to cut next. In contrast, three image compression algorithms described in this chapter, execute in $O(nlogn)$ for encoding, where n is the number of image pixels and there is no need to send side information while reconstructing the image. In addition, using triangles only, rather than more general n-gons ($3 \leq n \leq 8$) allows efficient binary coding of the decomposition tree [1].

Radha et. al. [11] presented a new image segmentation based image coding that divides the desired image using binary space partitioning (BSP). The BSP approach partitions the desired image recursively along arbitrarily oriented lines in a hierarchical manner. This recursive partitioning generates a binary tree, which is referred to as the BSP tree representation of the given image. The most critical aspect of the BSP tree method is the criterion used to select the partitioning lines. Samset [12] presented an exhaustive survey of the Quadtree and related hierarchical data structures. These are based on the principle of domain decomposition, where the image is divided into four equal sized quadrants. In rectangular mesh (quadtree encoding) orientation of rectangles are always the same resulting in the *blocky* artifact in the reconstructed image.

Babuska [13] presented a finite element procedure consists of finding an approximate solution in the form of piecewise linear functions or piecewise quadratic functions. For two dimensional problems, one of the most frequently used approaches is to triangulate the domain and find the approximate solution which is linear or quadratic within every triangle. An essential condition is that the internal angles of every triangle should not be too small or close to 180°. Rippa [14] concluded that triangles should be long in a direction where the magnitude of second order directional derivative of function F is small and thin in direction where the magnitude of the second directional derivative of F is large for a good piecewise linear interpolation of surfaces. Plaza et. al. [15] proved that the sequence of meshes constructed by applying a skeleton regular partition over each element of the preceding mesh have an associated set of difference equations which relate the number of elements, faces, edges and vertices of the nth and (n-1)th meshes. Mitchell [16] developed a method for approximating the maximum-angle triangulation. Their covering triangulation has minimum angle at least a constant times upper bound. The upper bound itself depends on local geometric features of the input.

The coding schemes described in this chapter are based on domain decomposition and linear interpolation. The decomposition schemes involve triangulating the domain recursively. Linear interpolation has been chosen since, while yielding an acceptable quality in the coded image, it has a convenient computational cost compared to other methods [17–21]. The interpolation performed by the proposed coding methods requires only four floating-point multiplications and one floating-point division per pixel. As a result, it runs much faster than the standard techniques based on transforms [22–25].

2.2 Introduction

Scattered data interpolation in R^2 consists of constructing a function $F_A = F_A(x, y)$ such that

$$F_A(x_i, y_i) = f_i \qquad i = 1, \ldots \ldots, N$$

where $V = \{v_i = (x_i, y_i) \in R^2, i = 1, \ldots, N\}$ is a set of distinct and non-collinear data points and $f = (f_1, \ldots, f_n)$ is a (real) data vector. Usually we assume that the data vector f is sampled from some underlying function F and we wish to get a good approximation to F by F_A. A widely used method is to construct a triangulation T of V and to define the interpolating surface to be a linear function on each of the triangles of T.

Definition (*Conforming Triangulation*): Let Ω be any bounded domain in R^2 or R^3 with no-empty interior and polygonal boundary $\partial\Omega$, and consider a partition of Ω into a set of triangles $\tau = \{t_1, t_2, t_3, \ldots, t_n\}$. Then we say that τ is conforming triangulation if the following properties hold:

1. $\Omega = \bigcup t_i$
2. *interior* $(t_i) \neq \varphi$, $\forall t_i \in \tau$
3. *interior* $(t_i) \cap$ *interior* $(t_j) = \varphi$, if $i \neq j$
4. $\forall t_i, t_j \in \tau$ with $t_i \cap t_j \neq \varphi$, then $t_i \cap t_j$ is an entire face or a common edge, or a common vertex.

Definition (*Simplex*): A closed subset $T \subset R^n$ is called a (k)-simplex, $0 \leq k \leq n$ if T is the convex hull of $k + 1$ vertices $x^0, x^1, x^2, \ldots\ldots\ldots, x^k \in R^n$.

$$T = \left[x^{(0)}, x^{(1)}, x^{(2)}, \ldots\ldots\ldots, x^{(k)} \right] :$$
$$= \left\{ \sum_{j=0}^{k} \lambda_j x^{(j)} \mid \sum_{j=0}^{k} \lambda_j = 1, \quad \lambda_j \in [0, 1], \; 0 \leq j \leq k \right\}$$

If $k = n$ then T is simply called simplex or triangle in R^n.

Definition (*Compression Ratio*): Compression Ratio (*Cr*) is defined as

$$Cr = \frac{\text{Number of bits required for representing the image before compression}}{\text{Number of bits required for representing the image after compression}}$$

Definition (*Peak Signal to Noise Ratio*): Peak Signal to Noise Ratio (PSNR) is defined as

$$Peak\,Signal\,to\,Noise\,Ratio = 10\log_{10} \frac{PeakSignal^2}{MSE}$$

$$Mean\,Square\,Error\,(MSE) = \frac{1}{MN} \sum_{1}^{M} \sum_{1}^{N} (F(x, y) - F'(x, y))^2$$

$F(x,y)$ and $F'(x,y)$ represent gray values of M x N original and reconstructed image and the peak signal is the highest gray value in the image.

Fig. 2.1 3D triangles
B approximate the intensity
surface *A*. Corresponding 2D
Triangles are projections on
the XY plane

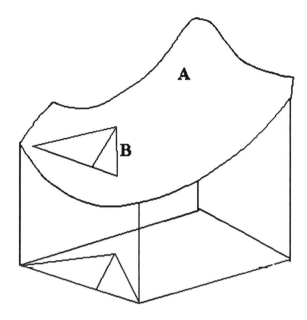

2.3 Coding Scheme

The image to be encoded can be regarded as a discrete surface i.e. a finite set of points in three dimensional (3-D) space, by considering a nonnegative discrete function of two variables $F(x, y)$ and establishing the correspondence between the image and the surface $A = \{(x, y, c)| c = F(x, y)\}$, so that each point in A corresponds to a pixel in the image: the couple (x, y) gives the pixel's position in the XY plane, while c (the point's height) is the pixel's gray value.

Our goal is to approximate A by a discrete surface $B = \{(x, y, d)| d = G(x, y)\}$, defined by means of a finite set of points. *3DT* means a triangle in 3-D, and *2DT* means a triangle in 2-D (usually, projection of 3DT on XY plane). Figure 2.1. shows a region of the surface A being approximated by two 3DTs [1]. The corresponding 2DTs are shown in the XY plane. Let T be a generic *2DT* the XY plane comprising of vertices:

$$P_1 = (x_1, y_1), \ P_2 = (x_2, y_2), \ P_3 = (x_3, y_3) \tag{2.1}$$

And let

$$c_1 = F(x_1, y_1), \quad c_2 = F(x_2, y_2), \quad c_3 = F(x_3, y_3)$$

represent the gray values at P_1, P_2, and P_3 respectively such that

$$(x_1, y_1, c_1), (x_2, y_2, c_2), (x_3, y_3, c_3) \in A. \tag{2.2}$$

The gray value prediction function G is given by the linear interpolation of the gray values at the triangle vertices:

$$G(x, y) = c_1 + \alpha(c_2 - c_1) + \beta(c_3 - c_1) \tag{2.3}$$

Where α and β are defined by the two relations [1]:

$$\alpha = \frac{(x - x_1)(y_3 - y_1) - (y - y_1)(x_3 - x_1)}{(x_2 - x_1)(y_3 - y_1) - (y_2 - y_1)(x_3 - x_1)} \tag{2.4}$$

$$\beta = \frac{(x_2 - x_1)(y - y_1) - (y_2 - y_1)(x - x_1)}{(x_2 - x_1)(y_3 - y_1) - (y_2 - y_1)(x_3 - x_1)} \tag{2.5}$$

From this definition, it can be seen that the values of F and G coincide at the vertices of T:

$$F(P_1) = G(P_1); \; F(P_2) = G(P_2); \; F(P_3) = G(P_3) \tag{2.6}$$

The prediction function G can be tested by defining

$$Err(x, y) = |F(x, y) - G(x, y)| \tag{2.7}$$

And checking for the condition

$$Err(x, y) \leq e \tag{2.8}$$

Here, $e > 0$ is an adjustable quality factor.

2.3.1 Binary Tree Triangular Coding (BTTC) Scheme

The BTTC algorithm given by Distasi [1] is based on the recursive decomposition of image domain into right-angled isosceles triangles arranged in a binary tree. The gray values are approximated using the Eqs. (2.1) to (2.8) that compute linear interpolation of gray values at the triangle vertices.

If condition (2.8) does not hold, the triangle T is divided into two triangles by dividing along its height relative to the hypotenuse as shown in Fig. 2.2a. In this way, the resulting triangles are always right angled. If the sub division procedure is reiterated indefinitely, we eventually obtain a minimal triangle comprising of only three adjacent pixels, namely their vertices which satisfy the condition (2.8), since the equalities in (2.6) ensure that Err $(x, y) = 0$ on each of the three vertices. The relevant information known as topological information is stored in a hierarchical structure- a binary tree. Figure 2.2b shows how the partition process works: each time a triangle is subdivided the resulting triangles become its children in the tree. Hence, each node has either zero or two children. The pseudo code of BTTC is given in Sect. 2.3.1.1.

It is assumed that the image is square shaped and has side length m, where $m = 2^k + 1$ for some integer $k \geq 1$, if this is not the case the image is suitably padded. With this assumption, all the triangles generated by subsequent divisions

Fig. 2.2 a. Example of
domain partition process
using BTTC **b.** Tree
representation of the
decomposition

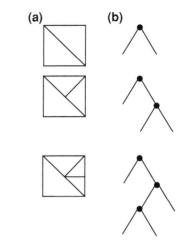

Fig. 2.3 Possible domain
partition and the resulting
binary string *S* using BTTC.
Only *underlined* substring has
to be stored

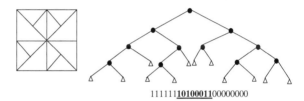

111111**1010001**100000000

will be isosceles and their hypotenuse's length in pixels will be of the form
$(2^h + 1)$ for some $h \geq 1$ Fig. 2.3.

Distasi [1] represents a triangle of vertices P_1, P_2, P_3 by $\langle P_1 P_2 P_3 \rangle$. The first
vertex corresponds to the right angle; the other two vertices follow clockwise. The
structure of the resulting B tree is stored in a binary string S obtained from a
breadth-first visit of the tree: the value 0 represents a leaf node, the value 1 an
intermediate node; the root is not stored at all. In this way, one needs a single bit
for each node (with the exception of the root). If p is the minimum level at which a
leaf appears, one can avoid storing all the leading 1's if a track of p is kept. This
removes a redundant substring of 1's with a length $\sum_{i=1}^{p-1} 2^i = 2^p - 2$.

Similarly, if r is the B tree's maximum depth, all the trailing 0's need not be
stored because leaves at level r can be inferred knowing which non-leaf nodes are
at level r-1. In the case of a complete tree with $r + 1$ levels numbered from 0 to r,
2^r nodes out of $2^{r+1} - 1$ can be spared by Distasi's coding, but in the worst case one
only saves the storage space for two leaves. The pixel gray values of the triangle
vertices are stored after the binary string S.

Fig. 2.4 Representation of
three triangle partition, A is
the point of maximum
prediction error

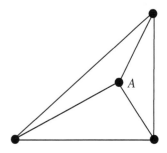

2.3.1.1 Binary Tree triangular Coding (BTTC) Algorithm [1]

//L is list of leaves with no further processing

1. Set $L = NULL$;

   Set $T_1 = \; <(1,1)(1,m)(m,1)> , T_2 = \; <(m,m)(m,1)(1,m)> .$

2. Push T_1 and T_2 into stack.
3. Pop the Triangle T from stack.

   Let $P_1 = (x_1, y_1), P_2 = (x_2, y_2), P_3 = (x_3, y_3)$ be it's vertices.
   Set $C_1 = F(x_1, y_1), C_2 = F(x_2, y_2), C_3 = F(x_3, y_3)$.

4. For each pixel $(x,y) \in T$, calculate $G(x,y)$ using (2.3),(2.4) and (2.5). If $Err(x,y) = |F(x,y) - G(x,y)|$ does not exceed user defined quality factor (e) then go to step 6.
5. Set $P_{max} = (P_2 + P_3)/2$; Set $T_1 = \; <P_{max}P_3P_1> , T_2 = \; <P_{max}P_1P_2>$
   Go to step 2.
6. Insert T into L.
7. If the stack is empty then stop, otherwise go to step 3.

   In the following Sections, we introduce three modifications to the BTTC by placing a new vertex at the point of maximum prediction error. All these algorithms result in significant reduction in depth of recursion while offering image quality comparable to BTTC.

2.3.2 Three Triangle Decomposition Scheme

Definition (*Three-Triangle Partition*): The three-triangle partition of triangle T is defined as follows:

1. Add a new node A, at point of maximum prediction error in the triangle T [26]
2. Join the node A with every vertex of triangle T as shown in Fig. 2.4.

Fig. 2.5 a Example of the
new domain partition process
using three triangle
decomposition scheme,
b Tree representation of the
decomposition

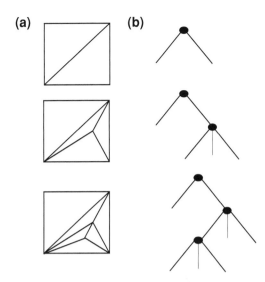

Initially, the image is divided into two triangles by drawing the diagonal. Then the triangle T is divided into three triangles by placing a new vertex at the point of maximum prediction error and connecting it to the three vertices of T as shown in Fig. 2.5a if Err (x, y) exceeds e. The process is repeated indefinitely, we eventually obtain triangles comprising only three adjacent pixels, which are the vertices surely satisfying Eq. (2.8) since inequalities in Eq. (2.6) ensure that Err $(x, y) = 0$ at each of these vertices.

The relevant topological information is stored in a hierarchical structure—a tree, a node represents each triangle whose position in the tree implicitly defines the vertex coordinates. Figure 2.5b shows how the partition process works: each time a triangle is subdivided the resulting triangles becomes its children in the tree. Hence, each node has either zero or three children. If maximum error point falls on any one of the edges then the node will have only two children. A triangle of vertices P_1, P_2, P_3 is represented by notation $<P_1P_2P_3>$. The pseudo code is given in Sect. 2.3.2.1.

2.3.2.1 Three Triangle Decomposition Algorithm

//L is the list of leaves that require no further processing
//m represents image size

1. *//*Initialize the set of "leaf" 2DT s

   Set $L = NULL$;
   *//*Initialize the first two-2DT s
   Set $T_1 = <(1, 1)(1, m)(m, 1)>, T_2 = <(m, m)(m, 1)(1, m)>$.

2. Push T_1 and T_2 into stack.
3. Pop the 2DT T from stack.

   Let $P_1 = (x_1, y_1), P_2 = (x_2, y_2), P_3 = (x_3, y_3)$ be its vertices.
   //Determine the 3DT corresponding to T
   Set $c_1 = F(x_1, y_1), c_2 = F(x_2, y_2), c_3 = F(x_3, y_3)$.

4. Calculate the point $P_m = (x_m, y_m)$ within the triangle T where the error is maximum.
5. //Test if the approximation for T is good enough

   If Eq. (2.8) is satisfied for each pixel in the triangle, then go to step 7.

6. //Divide T into three 2DT s by placing the vertex at the point of maximum error

   Set $P_{max} = (x_{max}, y_{max})$.
   Set $T1 = \ <P_{max}P_3P_1> , T2 = \ <P_{max}P_1P_2> , T3 = \ <P_2P_3P_{max}>$
   Push T_1, T_2, and T_3 into the stack.
   Go to step 3.

7. Insert T into L.
8. If the stack is empty then stop, otherwise go to step 3.

This new algorithm does not require the assumptions of BTTC [1]. The image need not be square shaped and the side length need not be of the form $m = 2^k + 1$ for some integer $k \geq 1$. The domain decomposition triangles need not be right-angled isosceles, but their shapes are determined by the distribution of gray values in the image. By placing the new vertex at the point of maximum error, we get less number of decompositions (lower average depth of recursion), or for the same number of decomposition the quality of the reconstructed image is significantly improved.

The resulting tree structure is shown in Fig. 2.6; and is stored in a binary string S obtained from the breath-first traversal of the tree. The root is not stored at any instance, the value 0 represents leaf node and the value 1 an intermediate node. Hence, one bit is needed for each node (with exception of the root). We can avoid storing all the leading 1's if we keep track of p, where p denotes the minimum level at which the leaf appears. If r is maximum depth of the tree, we can eliminate the storing of 0's that represents leaves at level r. The non-leaf nodes at level $r-1$ can give us the information about these leaves.

The gray values of the 3DT vertices are stored after the binary string S. Decoding is analogous to encoding, with the only difference being that the quality of approximation need not be tested.

In the first step of decoding the binary string S helps in the reconstruction of the tree structure. To implement this, the first two 2DTs (the biggest ones) are pushed into stack. The scanning of S is then done bit by bit from left to right. On encountering a 1 bit, the triangle under consideration is subdivided, and its three children triangles are pushed into stack; if the encountered bit is 0, the triangle under consideration is added to the list of leaves L.

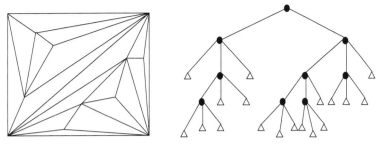

11**0101101001100000**000000000

Fig. 2.6 Possible domain partition with its tree and the resulting binary string S using three—triangle decomposition. Only the underlined substring has to be stored

The second step of decoding involves the generation of 3DT's from the gathered information. First, the pixels that have been marked in the reconstructed image receive their height along z direction (gray values); this defines F at the 2DT's vertices. Finally, Eq. (2.3) is computed inside each 2DT in L, thus reconstructing approximate surface B.

Proposition: Let τ_0 be any initial conforming triangulation with N_0 vertices, E_0 edges and T_0 triangles. Then after n applications, partition to each of the triangle τ_0 and its descendants, produce a globally refined and conforming triangulation τ_n. The number of nodes, edges and triangles in τ_n (respectively, N_n, E_n, T_n) are related with the number of elements in the preceding triangulation τ_{n-1} by means of the following equations:

$$\left. \begin{array}{l} N_n = N_{n-1} + T_{n-1} \\ E_n = E_{n-1} + 3T_{n-1} \\ T_n = 3T_{n-1} \end{array} \right\} \tag{2.9}$$

2.3.3 Interpolation Error

Interpolation on a triangular mesh constructs a function that attempts to approximate some "true" function, whose exact identity may not be known [14–16, 27, 28]. If a triangulation's sole purpose is as a basis for interpolation, the primary criterion of its fitness is how much the interpolated function differs from the true function. There are two types of interpolating errors: the difference between the interpolated function and the true function, and the difference between the gradients of the interpolated function and the true function.

Table 2.1 Bounds on interpolation error for a single element t

	$\|f - g\|_\infty$	$\|\nabla f - \nabla g\|_\infty$
Upper bound, triangles	$c_t r_{mc}^2$	$c_t \frac{l_{max} l_{med} (l_{mid} + 4 r_{in})}{2A}$
Weaker but simple upper bound, triangles	$c_t \frac{r_{max}^2}{3}$	$c_t \frac{3 l_{max} l_{med} l_{mid}}{2A} = c_t \frac{l_{max}}{\sin \theta_{max}} = 2 c_t r_{circ}$
Lower bound, triangles	$c_t r_{mc}^2$	$2 c_t \max \int r_{circ}, \alpha_{max}, \sqrt{l_{max}^2 - \alpha_{med}^2}$

All bounds assume that the magnitude of the directional second derivative of f does not exceed $2c_t$

Let T be a triangular mesh and let $f(p)$ be a continuous scalar function defined over the mesh. Let $g(p)$ be a piecewise linear approximation to $f(p)$, where $g(v) = f(v)$ at each vertex v of T. Table 2.1 gives bounds on two types of interpolation error associated with g. The norm $\|f - g\|_\infty$ is defined as the maximum pointwise interpolation error over the element t, $\max_{p \in t} |f(p) - g(p)|$. The norm $\|\nabla f - \nabla g\|_\infty$ is maximum magnitude of the pointwise error in the interpolated gradient, $\max_{p \in t} |\nabla f(p) - \nabla g(p)|$.

A	The signed area of triangle
l_1, l_2, l_3	The edge length of a triangle
l_{rms}	The root-mean-square edge length of a triangle $\sqrt{\frac{1}{3} \sum_{i=1}^{3} l_i^2}$
$l_{min}, l_{med}, l_{max}$	The minimum, median, and maximum edge lengths of an element
$\alpha_{med}, \alpha_{max}$	The median and maximum magnitude signed altitudes of a triangle $\alpha_{med} = 2A/l_{med}$ and $\alpha_{max} = 2A/l_{min}$
r_{circ}	The signed circumradius of an element
r_{in}	The signed inradius of an element $r_{in} = 2A/(l_{min} + l_{med} + l_{max})$
r_{mc}	The unsigned radius of min-containment circle
θ_i	The angle at vertex v_i of triangle
$\theta_{max}, \theta_{min}$	The signed minimum and maximum angles of a triangle

If $f(p)$ is arbitrary, $g(p)$ can be an arbitrarily bad approximation of $f(p)$. The error can be bounded only if $f(p)$ is constrained in some way. A reasonable constraint, which yields the error bounds in Table 2.1, is to assume that $f(p)$ is smooth and absolute curvature of $f(p)$ is bounded in each triangle t by some constant $2c_t$ (where c_t may differ for each t).

The upper bound on $\|f - g\|_\infty$, the maximum interpolation error over t, is $c_t r_{mc}^2$. This bound is tight for any triangle t with min-containment radius r_{mc} there is a function f such that $\|f - g\|_\infty = c_t r_{mc}^2$. This bound was first derived by Waldron [28] and it applies to higher-dimensional simple elements as well. It is interesting to compare this bound to the bounds usually given for interpolation, which implicate the maximum edge length of each element. To obtain a specified level of accuracy, a mesh is refined until no edge is larger than a specified length. However, the min-containment radius of an element gives a tighter bound on $\|f - g\|_\infty$ than the maximum edge length. Unfortunately, the min-containment radius r_{mc} is expensive to compute. The maximum edge length l_{max} is much faster alternative and for a triangle $r_{mc} \leq l_{max}/\sqrt{3}$. The substitution yields the faster-to-compute but slightly looser bounds $\|f - g\|_\infty \leq c_t l^2_{max}/3$.

The error (f-g) is not the only concern. In many applications, g is expected to accurately represent the gradients of f, and the error $\nabla f - \nabla g$ is just as important, or more important than (f-g).

The bounds reveal that $\|\nabla f - \nabla g\|_\infty$ can grow arbitrarily large as elements become arbitrarily badly shaped, unlike $\|f - g\|_\infty$. Observe that the area appears in the denominator of these bounds. Imagine distorting a triangle so that its area approaches zero. Then ∇g may or may not approach infinity, depending on whether the numerator of the error bound also approaches zero. First, consider an isosceles triangle with one angle approaching 180° and two tiny triangles. As the large angle approaches 180°, A approaches zero and the edge lengths do not change much, so the error bounds grow arbitrarily large. Now imagine an isosceles triangle with one tiny angle and two angles near 90°. As tiny angles approach zero, A approaches zero, but l_{min} and r_{in} approach zero at the same rate, so the error bound does not change much. Hence, angles near 180 are harmful to good triangulation.

Lemma 2.1: *At any vertex V of triangulation with all angles at least* α,

$$\frac{|E|}{|F|} \leq k^{\angle EF/\alpha}$$

Where E and F are edges at V, and k = 2cos. Note $1 \leq k < 2$ *and* $\angle EF\alpha/ \geq 1$.

Proof We use induction on the number of edges between E and F at V. The base case is if there are no edges between E and F, that is if E and F are in a common triangle T. Let G be the third edge and e, f, and g the angles opposite E, F and G.

From the law of *sines*, $|E|/|F| = \sin e / \sin f$. This may be expressed as $\sin(g+f)/\sin f = \cos g + \sin g \cos f / \sin f$. For any triangle θ we have $\pi > \theta \geq \alpha$, which implies $\cos \theta \leq \cos \alpha$. Hence the above is less than $(k/2)(1 + \sin g/\sin f)$.

If $f > g$, then this is less than k. Otherwise, the worst case is when $f = \alpha$. If $g = \alpha$ as well, then the above equals α. Furthermore, since $\sin (g + \alpha)/\sin \alpha$ is a more slowly growing function of g than is $k^{g/\alpha}$, we have that $\sin(g + \alpha) / \sin\alpha < k^{g/\alpha}$ for all $g > \alpha$.

For the induction step, let H be any edge between E and F. By induction, the theorem is true for the number of edges between E and H and between H and F. Thus

$$\frac{|E|}{|F|} = \frac{|E|}{|H|}\frac{|H|}{|F|} \leq k^{\angle EH}k^{\angle HF} = k^{\angle EF}$$

Definition (*Wedges*): Triangulate part of P by introducing sequence of triangles called wedges at vertices of P, where P is a general polygon.

Theorem 2.1 Any wedge with edges E and F has smallest angle

Fig. 2.7 Three, Six and
Nine-domain triangulation
for image lisaw (e = 13). The
triangulations are shown at an
intermediate stage of the
algorithm

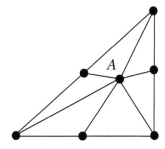

$$\leq \min\left(\angle EF, \angle EF / \log \frac{|E|}{|F|}\right)$$

Proof The contrapositive of lemma 2.1 is that a wedge has an angle less than α
whenever

$$k^{\angle EF/\alpha} < \frac{|E|}{F}$$

This condition is satisfied for any $\alpha > \angle EF / \log(|E|/|F|)$. Taking the limit as α
approaches the right hand side, the wedge has an angle $\leq \angle EF / \log(|E|/|F|)$. The
proof is completed by also noting that no wedge can have smallest angle between
two of its edges, $\angle EF$.

Advantage of three triangle decomposition algorithm is converting the point of
maximum error value to be the point of zero error value by making it a vertex of
the triangle, so the quality of the image is bound to improve. Disadvantage is this
forms too many thin triangles in late stages of decomposition. This results in many
predicted values being affected by gray value of a vertex which is very far from the
pixel under consideration as shown in Fig. 2.7a. After several simulation experi-
ments we introduced a modification to control the production of thin triangles by
decomposing original triangle into six new triangles making them more regular
instead of thin slices as mentioned in Sect. 2.3.3. Although several heuristics can
be used in the implementation of six triangle decomposition method, the following
subsection shows the six triangle method using one of the heuristic.

2.3.4 Six Triangle Decomposition Scheme

Definition (*Six-Triangle Partition*): The six-triangle partition of triangle T is
defined as follows [26]

1. Add a new node A at point of maximum prediction error in the triangle T and
   new nodes at the midpoints of the edges of T.

Fig. 2.8 Representation of six triangle partition

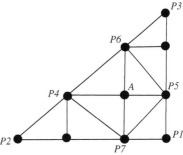

$$x_4^{i+1} = ((x_2^i - x_3^i)/(y_2^i - y_3^i))*(y^i - y_2^i) + x_2^i$$
$$x_5^{i+1} = x_1^i$$
$$x_6^{i+1} = x^i$$
$$x_7^{i+1} = x^i$$
$$y_4^{i+1} = y^i$$
$$y_5^{i+1} = y^i$$
$$y_6^{i+1} = ((y_2^i - y_3^i)/(x_2^i - x_3^i))*(x^i - x_2^i) + y_2^i$$
$$y_7^{i+1} = x1^i$$

Where (x^i, y^i) is the point of maximum error and i is the recursive index

2. Join the node A with every vertex of triangle T and the nodes over the boundary of T as shown in Fig. 2.8.

2.3.4.1 Six Triangle Decomposition Algorithm

1. Divide the image into two right-angled triangles.
2. Push the triangles on the stack.
3. Pop a triangle from the stack

   a. Calculate error values for all points inside the triangle (using prediction formula).
   b. If error $\leq e$ for each pixel in the triangle, write the triangle in a file.
   c. Else decompose the triangle into six new triangles by first joining the point of maximum error with the three vertices of the original triangle and then by joining the point of maximum error with the midpoints of the opposite sides of the three new triangles.
   d. Push the six new triangles on the stack. Repeat step 3 for all the remaining triangles in the stack.

Advantage of this algorithm is the number of thin triangles formed was greatly reduced and there was improvement in the quality of images. In six-triangle method by drawing the medians, we observed that there was no uniformity/regularity in the pattern formation of new triangles as shown in Fig. 2.7b.

Proposition: *For six triangle partition, the number of nodes, edges and triangles of refined mesh τ_n (respectively, N_n, E_n, T_n) are related with the number of elements in the preceding triangulation τ_{n-1} by means of the following equations:*

$$\left.\begin{array}{l} N_n = N_{n-1} + T_{n-1} + E_{n-1} \\ E_n = 2E_{n-1} + 6T_{n-1} \\ T_n = 6T_{n-1} \end{array}\right\} \qquad (2.10)$$

Improvement of this algorithm is nine triangle decomposition. In nine triangle method we draw the perpendiculars instead of medians. To implement nine triangle decomposition method several heuristics can be used. The nine triangle method using one of the heuristic is shown in the following subsection.

2.3.5 Nine Triangle Decomposition Scheme

Definition (*Nine-Triangle Partition*): The nine-triangle partition of triangle T is defined as follows [26]

1. Let P_1, P_2, and P_3 be the vertex of the original triangle and A is the point inside the triangle. Draw perpendiculars passing through A along x and y-axis so that they cut the triangle at points P_4, P_5, P_6, P_7.
2. Draw perpendicular from the two new points (P_4, P_6) on the sides of the triangle as shown in Fig. 2.9.
3. Join the end points of the first two perpendiculars so as to form a total of nine triangles inside the original triangle.

This construction utilizes the information about the point of maximum prediction error and yet results in relatively regular domain decomposition that avoids thin slices.

$$x_4^{i+1} = \left((x_2^i - x_3^i)/(y_2^i - y_3^i)\right)^* (y^i - y_2^i) + x_2^i$$
$$x_5^{i+1} = x_1^i$$
$$x_6^{i+1} = x^i$$
$$x_7^{i+1} = x^i$$
$$y_4^{i+1} = y^i$$
$$y_5^{i+1} = y^i$$
$$y_6^{i+1} = \left((y_2^i - y_3^i)/(x_2^i - x_3^i)\right) * (x^i - x_2^i) + y_2^i$$
$$y_7^{i+1} = x1^i$$

Where (x^i, y^i) is the point of maximum error and i is the recursive index.

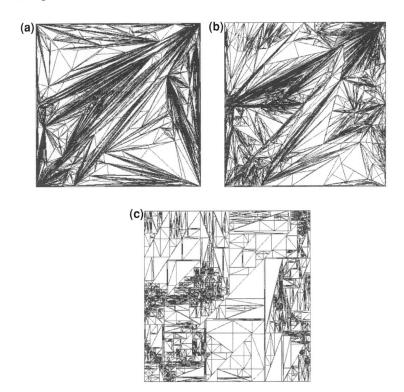

Fig. 2.9 Nine-triangle Decomposition: geometry and recursive relations that defines the decomposition. *A* is point of maximum prediction error

2.3.5.1 Nine Triangle Decomposition Algorithm

1. Divide the image into two right-angled triangles.
2. Push the triangles on the stack
3. Pop a triangle from the stack

   a. Calculate error values for all points inside the triangle (using prediction formula)
   b. If error $\leq$ e for each pixel in the triangle, write the triangle in a file.
   c. Else, decompose the triangle into nine new triangles by using the equations given in Fig. 2.9.
   d. Push the nine new triangles on the stack.

   Repeat step 3 for all the remaining triangles in the stack.

Proposition: *The number of nodes, edges and triangles of refined mesh* τ_n *(respectively,* N_n, E_n, T_n*) are related with the number of elements in the preceding triangulation* τ_{n-1}, *for nine triangle partition, by means of the following equations:*

$$\left.\begin{array}{l} N_n = N_{n-1} + 2E_{n-1} + T_{n-1} \\ E_n = 3E_{n-1} + 9T_{n-1} \\ T_n = 9T_{n-1} \end{array}\right\} \tag{2.11}$$

In general, any skeleton-regular simplex partition in 2D has associated set of difference constitutive equations:

$$\left.\begin{array}{l} N_n = N_{n-1} + aE_{n-1} + bT_{n-1} \\ E_n = cE_{n-1} + dT_{n-1} \\ T_n = eT_{n-1} \end{array}\right\} \tag{2.12}$$

Where the parameters a, b, c, d, e are determined by the specific partition and respectively, correspond to the number of nodes per edge, the number of internal nodes per triangle, the number of son-edges per edge, the number of inter edges per triangle, and the number of son triangles per triangle.

Theorem 2.2: For any 2D conforming triangulation having N_n nodes, E_n edges, and T_n triangles, the average number of triangles by node and edges by node are given as follows:

$$\text{Av\#(triangles per node)} = \frac{3T_n}{N_n}$$

$$\text{Av\#(edges per node)} = \frac{2E_n}{N_n}$$

Proof: Let us consider first the average of triangles per node. Since we are calculating an average per node, the denominator has to be N_n. The numerator in exchange is

$$\sum_{i=1}^{n} n_T(i),$$

Where $n_T(i)$ represents the number of triangles sharing node i. However, since this sum is equal to the sum of the number of nodes per triangle, it follows that

$$\sum_{i=1}^{n} n_T(i) = 3T_n$$

For the average number of edges per node the reasoning is the same.

2.3.5.2 Computing Time

The three, six, and nine triangle compression algorithms have proven to be time efficient. For encoding, it requires a computing time proportional to n, where n is

Fig. 2.10 Every triangle of a
Delaunay triangulation has an
empty circumcircle

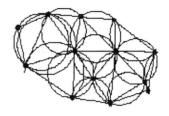

number of pixels in the image. The recurrence relation for nine-triangle method
gives the computing time:

$$T(n) = a, \qquad\qquad \text{for } n = 1, \text{ where a is a constant}$$
$$= 9\,T(n/9) + cn, \qquad \text{for } n > 1, \text{ where c is constant}$$

If n is a power of 9, $n = 9^{k}$ we can solve this equation by successive substi-
tutions, namely,

$$
\begin{aligned}
T(n) &= 9(9T\,(n/81) + (cn/9)) \\
&= 81T(n/81) + cn \\
&= \ldots\ldots = 9^{k}T(1) + kcn \\
&= an + cn\log n
\end{aligned}
$$
$$\text{Therefore}\quad T(n) \qquad = O(n\log n)$$

As it is easy to see that if $9k < n \le 9^{k+1}$ then $T(n) \le T\left(9^{k+1}\right)$.

Decoding is same as encoding; with the only difference being that the quality of
the approximation need not be tested. The first and second steps of the above
algorithm are performed in $\theta(t)$ time, where t is the number of nodes in the tree.
The final step, requiring a calculation of Eq. (2.3)–(2.5) for each pixel, can be
completed in $\theta(n)$ time. Since $t < n$, the total time for decompression is $\theta(n)$.

2.3.6 Delaunay Triangulation Scheme

Delaunay triangulation is the most prominent one among the Voronoi diagrams.
It contains edge connecting two sites in a plane if and only if their Voronoi
regions share a common edge. The structure was introduced by Voronoi for sites
that form a lattice. Delaunay [29] extended the structure for the irregularly
placed sites by means of empty circles method. Consider all triangles formed by
the sites such that the circumcircle of each triangle is empty of other sites as
shown in Fig. 2.10. The set of edges of these triangles gives the Delaunay
triangulation of the sites. Voronoi diagram and the Delaunay triangulation are
duals as shown in Fig. 2.11.

Fig. 2.11 Voronoi diagram
and Delaunay triangulation
are duals. *Solid lines* show
Delaunay triangulation and
dotted lines show Voronoi
diagram

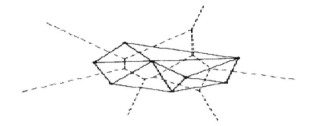

In the worst case, the time complexity of the Delaunay triangulation algorithm is $O(n^2)$ for given n sites [29]. Guibas et. al. [30] presented the Delaunay triangulation using Divide and Conquer techniques and the algorithm executes in $O(nlogn)$ time and that insert a new site in $O(n)$ time. Su et. al. [31] compared different sequential Delaunay triangulation algorithms: Divide and Conquer, Sweep line and incremental approach. They described a new version of the incremental algorithm that is simple to understand and implement. They also analyzed the major high level primitives used by each algorithm as well as how often each algorithm performs each operation. Shewchuk [32] presented the survey of Delaunay triangulation in two or more dimensions, their properties and several algorithms for constructing them and presented a brief survey of research in mesh generation. Special attention was given to methods based on Delaunay triangulation and tetrahedralization and to the methods that generate meshes as the guarantee of having favorable qualities.

S. Lertrattanapanich et. al. [33] proposed an algorithm based on spatial tessellation. They also proposed that the approximation of each triangle patch in Delaunay triangulation by a bivariate polynomial is advanced to construct a high resolution high quality image from a set of low resolution frames. Franck Davoine et. al. [34] presented a new scheme for fractal image compression based on adaptive Delaunay triangulation. Such a partition is computed on an initial set of points obtained with a split and merge algorithm in a gray level dependant way. The triangulation is thus fully flexible and returns a limited number of blocks allowing good compression ratio. This Section presents a new image compression algorithm using Delaunay triangulation and linear interpolation.

Consider initial lattice as shown in Fig. 2.12. The number of pixels between the any two rows and columns are 2^k, where $k > 1$. First pixel in the alternate rows is placed at a distance of $2^k/2$ and the remaining pixels in the same row are at a distance of 2^k. After constructing the initial lattice, Delaunay triangulation is performed using divide and conquer technique [30]. When the variance of any triangle in the triangular mesh is greater than user defined threshold, a new point at barycenter of the triangle is introduced and Delaunay procedure is performed again. The process is repeated, until all the triangles in the triangular mesh have their variance less than or equal to the threshold value. The Delaunay compression algorithm is given in Sect. 2.3.6.1. After compression, the final lattice and its corresponding gray values are stored.

Fig. 2.12 Initial lattice for
performing the Delaunay
triangulation

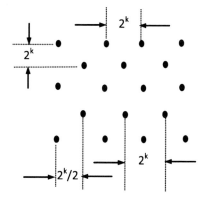

The decompression algorithm applies Delaunay triangulation on the stored
lattice and the remaining pixels in the triangle are computed by linear interpolation
using vertices gray values. The Delaunay decompression algorithm is given in
Sect. 2.3.6.2.

2.3.6.1 Delaunay Compression Algorithm

1. Construct initial lattice (triangle vertices)
2. Calculate the Delaunay triangulation of the set of vertices
3. For each triangle: if the variance of the triangle is greater than prefixed
   threshold then insert a vertex on its barycenter then goto step 2 else exit.

2.3.6.2 Delaunay Decompression Algorithm

1. Apply Delaunay triangulation on final lattice of points
2. For each triangle, interpolate the pixels using vertices gray values of the
   triangle.

2.3.6.3 Computing Time

In the worst case the first step of the compression algorithm executes in $O(n)$ time
and the second step executes in $O(nlogn)$ time. In the third step, the loop executes
in $O(n)$ time then all the pixels in the image will become the vertices of triangles.
Then the worst case time complexity of the Delaunay compression is $O(n^2logn)$
time, where n is the number of pixels in the image.

Fig. 2.13 Original lisaw
image

In Decompression algorithm the first step executes in $O(nlogn)$ and the second step executes in $O(n)$ time. So the time complexity of the decompression algorithm is $O(nlogn)$.

2.4 Experimental Results

All algorithms were coded in C and executed on Pentium III, 850 MHz machine. To evaluate the performance of nine-triangle method and Delaunay triangulation algorithm several standard 8 bit test images were used like lisaw 200 × 200, lenna 512 × 512, baboon 512 × 512 etc. The nine-triangle algorithm gives consistently better performance than three and six triangle decomposition algorithms on all test images we used. This Section presents some results obtained on such images— lisaw and lenna shown in Figs. 2.13 and 2.14. The visual results of the algorithm on lisaw and lenna compressed using nine-triangulation method at different levels of quality are illustrated in Figs. 2.15 and 2.16. Figure 2.7 shows the sample outcome of domain partition of this test image lisaw, at an intermediate stage of an algorithm.

Table 2.2 shows the test statistics obtained for the image lisaw 200 × 200. In Table 2.2 the first column specifies the quality factor e, while the following columns specify the height of the tree, CPU clock ticks required, Compression ratio, and Peak signal to noise ratio (PSNR). Table 2.3 shows the test result obtained for the image lenna 512 × 512. From the analysis of data in Table 2.2, it can be seen that height and computing time of nine triangular method is half of the BTTC as shown in Fig. 2.17a, b. The PSNR of nine triangle method is almost equal to BTTC and is slightly less than JPEG as shown in Fig. 2.17c and 2.18. It can be observed that as compression ratio increases, the PSNR values decreases. Low PSNR value means lower quality or the reconstructed image having more distortion. At low PSNR value, less number of triangles will be formed and less number of clock ticks required to compress the image. Visually, the quality of reconstructed image using nine-triangle coding is as good as JPEG. We tested the

Fig. 2.14 Reconstructed image lisaw at different compression ratios from *top left*: 2.54, 2.84, 3.78, and 5.27 using nine triangle decomposition

Fig. 2.15 Original lenna image

algorithms on various images from different application domain like medical images, satellite remote sensing images and industrial images—on all these test images similar conclusions can be drawn

Fig. 2.16 Reconstructed image lenna at different compression ratios from *top left*: 2.46, 2.79, 3.19, and 3.91 using nine triangle decomposition

Table 2.2 Distortion measures for image Lisaw

e	Height of the tree		Number of CPU clock ticks required		NINE		BTTC	
	NINE	BTTC	NINE	BTTC	COMPRESSION RATIO	PSNR	COMPRESSION RATIO	PSNR
2.2	5	14	145	319	2.54	32.79	1.07	33.63
4	5	13	132	318	2.84	32.73	1.27	33.47
6	4	12	115	273	3.78	32.47	2.68	33.45
8	4	12	102	258	5.27	32.03	4.76	33.34
11	4	11	92	253	7.37	31.27	8.00	32.11
13	4	10	87	239	8.94	30.51	10.22	31.43

The result of domain decomposition algorithm using Delaunay triangulation is given when $2^k = 32$. The domain decomposition of lenna using Delaunay triangulation is shown in Fig. 2.19. The visual results of the Delaunay compression

Table 2.3 Distortion measures for image lenna using BTTC, NINE and JPEG

e	PSNR		
	NINE	BTTC	JPEG
8.2	38.76	38.46	42.22
10	36.92	36.96	39.98
12	35.46	35.79	39.44
14	34.50	34.77	38.91
16	33.21	33.82	38.42
20	32.50	32.30	37.14
24	30.42	30.42	35.36
26	29.20	29.51	34.03

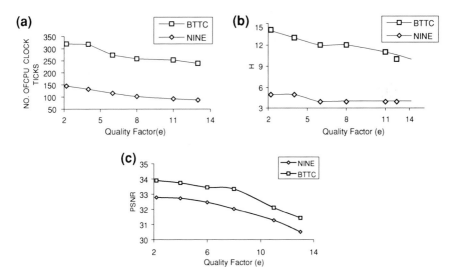

Fig. 2.17 Variation in **a** Number of CPU clock ticks, **b** Height (H) of domain partition tree, and **c** Peak-signal-to-noise-ratio for image lisaw. Note that lower e means higher quality

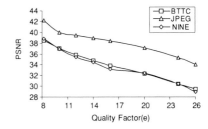

Fig. 2.18 Variation in peak-signal-to-noise-ratio for image Lenna. Note that lower e means higher image quality

algorithm on lenna at different levels of quality are illustrated in Fig. 2.20. It can be observed from Fig. 2.21 that the PSNR value at different compression ratios using image lenna is almost equal to BTTC and slightly less than JPEG. The time

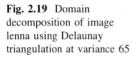

Fig. 2.19 Domain
decomposition of image
lenna using Delaunay
triangulation at variance 65

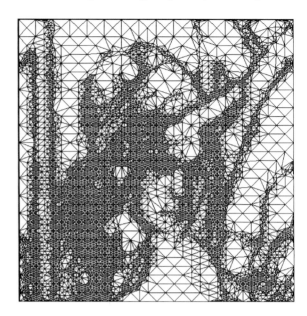

required to compress the given image by Delaunay triangulation is higher in
comparison to BTTC and JPEG as shown in Fig. 2.22.

2.5 Conclusions

This chapter presented four new lossy image decomposition algorithms for image
compression. The asymptotic time complexity of the three algorithms is O($nlogn$)
for coding and $\theta(n)$ for decoding. They are simple to implement and highly parallel. The algorithms are based on recursive domain triangulation and planar linear
interpolation between the vertices of the spatial triangles. Experimental results
show that the quality achieved is acceptable for the three-triangle algorithm and
the six-triangle algorithm and is very good for nine-triangle algorithm. The three
algorithms outperform BTTC with regard to execution time. Besides being sensitive to local features of the image, they maintain regularity of domain decomposition i.e. the domain decomposition is still recursive. Moreover, the three
algorithms relieve us from padding of image. What the three algorithms do is
simply decompose the image into new triangles irrespective of whether the new-
formed triangles are isosceles or not and exploit the point of maximum error.
However, since interpolation points are anchored at the point of maximum error,
these methods may be sensitive to noise, particularly if the variance of the noise is
very high. Delaunay triangulation has the property to maximize the minimum
angle. The algorithm executes in O(n^2logn) time for encoding and O($nlogn$) time
for decoding. The quality of the reconstructed image is almost equal to BTTC and

Fig. 2.20 Reconstructed image lenna at different compression ratios from *top left*: 4.08, 4.84, 5.33, and 5.83 using Delaunay triangulation compression algorithm

Fig. 2.21 Variation in PSNR using Delaunay triangulation for image lenna

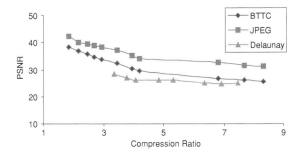

less than JPEG at similar compression ratios. The time taken is higher in comparison to BTTC and JPEG.

In this chapter, we have discussed four new image compression algorithms. The algorithms were implemented and their computational complexities were evaluated. In the next chapter, we introduce the domain decomposition based image

Fig. 2.22 Variation in
number of clock ticks using
Delaunay triangulation for
image lenna

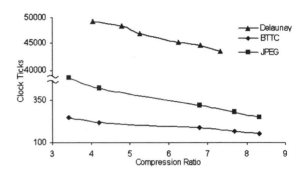

compression algorithms using fuzzy geometry measures and image quality measures.

References

1. Distasi R, Nappi M, Vitulano S (1997) Image compression by B-tree triangular coding. IEEE Trans Commun 45(9):1095–1100
2. Dimento LJ, Brekovich SY (1990) The compression effects of the binary tree overlapping method on digital imagery. IEEE Trans Commun 38:1260–1265
3. Radha H, Leonadi R, Vetterli M (1991) A multiresolution approach to binary tree representation of Images. Proc ICASSP 91:2653–2656
4. Strobach P (1989) Image coding based on quadtree–structured recursive least squares approximation. Proc IEEE ICAASP 89:1961–1964
5. Wu X (1992) Image coding by adaptive tree-structured segmentation. IEEE Trans Inf Theory 38(6):1755–1767
6. Davoine F, Svensson J, Chassery J-M (1995) A mixed triangular and quadrilateral partition for fractal image coding. In: Proceedings of the international conference on image processing (ICIP '95)
7. VC Da Silva, JM De Carvalho (2000) Image compression via TRITREE decomposition. In: Proceedings of the XIII Brazilian symposium on computer graphics and image processing (SIBGRAPI)
8. Li X, Knipe J, Cheng H (1997) Image compression and encryption using tree structures. Pattern Recogn Lett 18:1253–1259
9. Kotlov A (2001) Note: tree width and regular triangulations. Discret Math 237:187–191
10. Wu X, Fang Y (1995) A segmentation-based predictive multiresolution image coder. IEEE Trans Image Process 4:34–47
11. Radha H, Vetterli M, Leonardi R (1996) Image compression using binary space partitioning trees. IEEE Trans image process 5(12):1610–1623
12. Samet H (1984) The quadtree and related Hierarchical data structures. ACM Comput Surv 16(2):187–260
13. Babuska I, Aziz AK (1976) On the angle condition in the finite element method. Siam J Numer Anal 13(2):214–226
14. Rippa S (1992) Long and thin triangles can be good for linear interpolation. Siam J Numer Anal 29(1):257–270
15. Plaza A, Rivara M-C (2002) On the adjacencies of triangular meshes based on skeleton-regular partitions. J Comput Appl Math 140:673–693

16. Mitchell SA (1997) Approximating the maximum-angle covering triangulation. Comput Geom 7:93–111

17. Szelinski R (1990) Fast surface interpolation using hierarchical basis functions. IEEE Trans Pattern Anal Mach Intell 12:513–528

18. Vreelj B, Vaidyanathan PP (2001) Efficient implementation of all digital interpolation. IEEE Trans image process 10(11):1639–1646

19. Li J, Chen CS (2002) A simple efficient algorithm for interpolation between different grids in both 2D and 3D. Math Comput Sim 58:125–132

20. Chuah C-S, Leou J-J (2001) An adaptive image interpolation algorithm for image/video processing. Pattern Recogn 34:2383–2393

21. Boissonnant JD, Cazals F (2002) Smooth surface reconstruction via natural neighbour interpolation of distance functions. Comput Geom 22:185–203

22. Antonini M, Barlaud M, Mathieu P, Daubechies I (1992) Image coding using the wavelet transform. IEEE Trans Image Process 1(2):205–220

23. Vore BAD, Jawerth B, Lucien BJ (1992) Image compression through wavelet transform coding. IEEE Trans Inf Theory 38:719–746

24. Jacquin AE (1992) Image coding based on a fractal theory of iterated contractive image transformations. IEEE Trans Image Process 1:18–30

25. Helsingius M, Kuosmanen P, Astola J (2000) Image compression using multiple transforms. Signal Process Image Commun 15:513–529

26. Prasad MVNK, Mishra VN, Shukla KK (2003) Space partitioning based image compression using quality measures. Appl Soft Comput Elsevier Sci 3:273–282

27. Bramble JH, Zlamal M (1970) Triangular elements in the finite elements method. Math Comput 24(112):809–820

28. Waldron S (1998) The error in linear interpolation at the vertices of a simplex. Siam J Numer Anal 35:1191–1200

29. Aurenhammer F (1991) Voronoi diagrams—a survey of a fundamental geometric data structure. ACM Comput Surv 23(3):345–405

30. Guibas L, Stolfi J (1985) Primitives for the manipulation of general subdivisions and the computation of voronoi diagrams. ACM Trans Graph 4(2):74–123

31. Su P, Drysdale RLS (1995) A comparison of sequential delaunay triangulation algorithms, 11th Symposium computational geometry, Vancouver, B.C. Canada, pp 61–70

32. Shewchuk JR (1999) Lecture notes on delaunay mesh generation. University of California, Berkeley, p 20

33. Letrattanapanich S, Bose NK (2002) High resolution image formation from low resolution frames using delaunay triangulation. IEEE Trans Image Process 11(12):1427–1441

34. Davoine F, Antonini M, Chassery J-M, Barlaud M (1996) Fractal image compression based on delaunay triangulation and vector quantization. IEEE Trans Image Process 5(2):338–346

Chapter 3
Image Compression Using Quality Measures

Abstract This chapter discusses domain decomposition algorithms using quality measures like average difference, entropy, mean squared error and a fuzzy geometry measure called fuzzy compactness. All the partitioning methods discussed in this chapter execute in O($nlogn$) time for encoding and $\theta(n)$ time for decoding, where n is the number of pixels in the image.

Keywords Image quality · Average difference · Entropy · ME · Fuzzy sets · Fuzzy compactness

This chapter presents new partitioning methods for image compression using different image quality measures. These techniques are based on recursive partitioning of the image domain into right-angled triangles arranged in a binary tree. All the partitioning methods proposed in this chapter execute in O($nlogn$) time for encoding and $\theta(n)$ time for decoding, where n is the number of pixels in the image. Simulation results on standard test images show that the new methods produce significant improvement in quality when compared with conventional image compression techniques for comparable compression ratios. All these encoding techniques have faster execution time than JPEG, which requires O(n^2) time.

The general preliminaries are discussed in Sect. 3.1. Section 3.2 presents the new compression algorithms and their computational complexity. Experimental results of the domain decomposition algorithms are presented in Sect. 3.3. Finally, Sect. 3.4 concludes the chapter.

3.1 Space Decomposition

In space decomposition, the image is segmented into homogeneous regions. The segmentation process is carried out recursively and represented in the form of a binary tree structure. Different authors [1–7] have discussed segmentation-based

K. K. Shukla and M. V. Prasad, *Lossy Image Compression*,
SpringerBriefs in Computer Science, DOI: 10.1007/978-1-4471-2218-0_3,
© K. K. Shukla 2011

image coding (SIC). They demonstrated that SIC can be a very competitive alternative to established image coding techniques such as discrete cosine transform (DCT) and vector quantization (VQ). Astrid et al. [8] introduced the concept of hexagonal subsampled images. In hexagonally sampled images, a hierarchical subsampling structure is given which yields hexagon-like regions with fractal borders. Studies of hierarchical decompositions of hexagonally sampled images are biologically motivated since retina uses a hexagonal sampling pattern and human visual system utilizes pyramidal representations.

Da Silva et al. [5], presented a new method for image compression, using Tritree decomposition (TT). TT decomposition is similar to the Quadtree decomposition (QT), which has been broadly used by image processing algorithms, mainly for segmentation and compression. However, while QT subdivides the image into progressively smaller quadratic regions, TT decomposition subdivides the image in triangular regions. The goal is to segment the image into a set of triangular homogeneous regions, where the differences among the pixel values do not exceed a certain threshold. A tree is built to represent the decomposition. Each triangle will be a node of the TT tree. The initial triangle, that contains the whole image, is the root of the tree. The final triangles, representing the compressed image, are the leaves of the tree. Reconstruction of the image is accomplished by planar interpolation among the vertices of each triangle leaf. TT algorithm performs significantly better than QT.

Biswas et al. [9] described a hierarchical image segmentation scheme and its use in image compression. At each level of hierarchy, the segmentation provides a sub-image consisting of compact, homogeneous regions. A number of thresholds based on conditional entropy of the image guide the entire process. Very small regions are merged together. Objective measures based on correlation and contrasts have been proposed for evaluation of the segmentation technique, and the results of the proposed algorithm have been compared with those of three other multi-level thresholding algorithms.

Eckert et al. [10] presented a review of perceptual image quality metrics and their application to still image compression. The review describes how image quality metrics can be used to guide an image compression scheme and outlines the advantages, disadvantages and limitations of a number of quality metrics. They examine a broad range of metrics ranging from simple mathematical measures to those, which incorporate full perceptual models. They highlight some variation in the models for luminance adaptation and the contrast sensitivity function and discuss what appears to be a lack of a general consensus regarding the models which best describe contrast masking and error summation. They identify how the various perceptual components have been incorporated in quality metrics, and identify a number of psychophysical testing techniques that can be used to validate the metrics.

Davoine et al. [11] presented a new partitioning scheme for fractal image coding, based on triangles and quadrilaterals. The advantages of the triangles over the square and rectangular blocks are: adaptability to the image (reduction of the block effect), and to reduce the number of blocks by grouping neighboring triangles into quadrilaterals. Quadrilaterals permit a reduction in the number of local contractive affine transformations composing the fractal transform, and thus to increase the compression ratio, while preserving the visual quality of the decoded image.

3.1.1 Image Quality Measures

Eskicioglu et al. [12] evaluated several discrete bivariate image quality measures. They provide a measure of closeness between two digital images by exploiting the difference in the statistical distribution of pixel values. These measures use a distance function between corresponding pixel gray values in the original and reconstructed images. Consider an $M \times N$ image, where $M =$ number of pixel rows and $N =$ number of pixel columns. F(j,k) and $\hat{F}(j, k)$ denote the samples of original and reconstructed image gray values. The different quality measures can be divided into three groups and are listed in Table 3.1.

Group I: AD, SC
Group II: NK, CQ, LMSE, MD
Group III: WD, PMSE, IF, NAE, Normalized Mean Square Error (NMSE), L_p

Measures in Group I cannot be reliably used with all techniques, as the sign of the correlation function does not remain the same. Group II measures are consistent but have relatively poor correlation with human perception for some of the techniques. Among the useful measures in Group III NMSE is the best one for all kinds of test images.

3.1.2 Fuzzy Geometric Measures

In natural images, many features are associated with ambiguity or fuzziness. Several authors have used the fuzzy set concept for image processing [13–20]. Pal and Rosenfeld [14] have introduced several fuzzy geometric properties of images. They have used a fuzzy measure of image compactness for enhancement and thresholding.

Nobuhara et al. [21] have recently introduced the application of fuzzy relational equation to lossy image compression. Sinha et al. [22] introduced several fuzzy morphological algorithms for image processing tasks like shape detection, edge detection, and clutter removal.

A fuzzy subset of a set S is a mapping μ from S into [0,1]. For any $p \in S$, $\mu(p)$ is called the degree of membership of p in μ. The support of μ is an ordinary set and is defined as

$$S(\mu) = \{p \,|\, \mu(p) > 0\}$$

Table 3.1 Image Quality Measures

Average difference [12]	$AD = \sum_{j=1}^{M} \sum_{k=1}^{N} |F(j,k) - \hat{F}(j,k)| / MN$
Structural content [12]	$SC = \sum_{j=1}^{M} \sum_{k=1}^{N} [F(j,k)]^2 / \sum_{j=1}^{M} \sum_{k=1}^{N} [\hat{F}(j,k)]^2$
Normalized cross-correlation [12]	$NK = \sum_{j=1}^{M} \sum_{k=1}^{N} F(j,k)\hat{F}(j,k) / \sum_{j=1}^{M} \sum_{k=1}^{N} [\hat{F}(j,k)]^2$
Correlation quality [12]	$CQ = \sum_{j=1}^{M} \sum_{k=1}^{N} F(j,k)\hat{F}(j,k) / \sum_{j=1}^{M} \sum_{k=1}^{N} F(j,k)$
Maximum difference [12]	$MD = \mathrm{Max}(|F(j,k) - \hat{F}(j,k)|)$
Image fidelity [12]	$IF = 1 - \left(\sum_{j=1}^{M} \sum_{k=1}^{N} [F(j,k) - \hat{F}(j,k)]^2 / \sum_{j=1}^{M} \sum_{k=1}^{N} [F(j,k)]^2 \right)$
Weighted distance [12]	$WD = $ Every element of the difference matrix is normalized in some way and L_1 norm is applied.
Laplacian mean square error [12]	$LMSE = \sum_{j=1}^{M-1} \sum_{k=2}^{N-1} [O\{F(j,k)\} - O\{\hat{F}(j,k)\}]^2 / \sum_{j=1}^{M-1} \sum_{k=2}^{N-1} [O\{F(j,k)\}]^2$
Peak mean square error [12]	$PMSE = \frac{1}{MN} \left(\sum_{j=1}^{M} \sum_{k=1}^{N} [F(j,k) - \hat{F}(j,k)]^2 / \sum_{j=1}^{M} \sum_{k=1}^{N} [\mathrm{Max}\{F(j,k)\}]^2 \right)$
Normalized absolute error [12]	$NAE = \sum_{j=1}^{M} \sum_{k=1}^{N} [O\{F(j,k)\} - O\{\hat{F}(j,k)\}] / \sum_{j=1}^{M} \sum_{k=1}^{N} [O\{F(j,k)\}]$
Normalized mean square error [12]	$NMSE = \sum_{j=1}^{M} \sum_{k=1}^{N} [O\{F(j,k)\} - O\{\hat{F}(j,k)\}]^2 / \sum_{j=1}^{M} \sum_{k=1}^{N} [O\{F(j,k)\}]^2$
L_p-norm [12]	$L_p = \left\{ \frac{1}{MN} \sum_{j=1}^{M} \sum_{k=1}^{N} |F(j,k) - \hat{F}(j,k)|^p \right\}^{1/p}, p = 1,2,3$
Hosaka plot [12]	A graphical quality measure. The area and shape of the plot gives information about the type and amount of degradation.
Histogram [12]	Another graphical quality measure. Gives the probability distribution of the pixel values in the difference image.

For LSME, $O[F(j,k)] = F(j+1,k) + F(j-1,k) + F(j,k+1) + F(j,k-1) - 4F(j,k)$. For NAE, NMSE, and L_2-norm $O[F(j,k)]$ is defined in three ways: (1) $O[F(j,k)] = F(j,k)$, (2) $O[F(j,k)] = F(j,k)^{1/3}$ (3) $O[F(j,k)] = \{H(u^2 + v^2)\}^{1/2} F(u,v)$ (u, v are the coordinates in the transform domain)

p is called a cross-over point of μ if $\mu(p) = 0.5$. A crisp (ordinary, nonfuzzy) subset of S can be regarded as a special case of a fuzzy subset in which the mapping μ is into $\{0,1\}$.

Height: The height of a fuzzy set μ is defined as

$$h(\mu) = \int \max_{x}\{\mu(x,y)\}dy$$

where the integration is taken over a region outside which $\mu(x,y) = 0$

Width: Similarly the width of a fuzzy set is defined by

$$w(\mu) = \int \max_{y}\{\mu(x,y)\}dx$$

with the same condition over integration as above.

Length: The length of a fuzzy set μ is defined as

$$l(\mu) = \max_{x}\left\{\int \mu(x,y)dy\right\}$$

where the integration is taken over a region outside which $\mu(x,y) = 0$

Breadth: The breadth of a fuzzy set μ is defined as

$$b(\mu) = \max_{y}\left\{\int \mu(x,y)dx\right\}$$

where the integration is taken over a region outside which $\mu(x,y) = 0$

In the following sections, we develop image compression algorithms by using quality measures as a basis for image segmentation.

3.2 Coding Scheme

The BTTC [23–25] algorithm is based on the recursive decomposition of image domain into right-angled isosceles triangles arranged in a binary tree. The gray values are approximated using linear interpolation of gray values at the triangle vertices. The weakness of this algorithm is that in step 4 it uses an ad hoc error measure which is simply the absolute difference between actual and predicted value at a single pixel. Better triangulation can be expected if we use a widely accepted image quality measure to implement the subdivision in step 4 of the algorithm. In this chapter, we have used four different quality measures for this purpose and compared the performance of resulting image compression algorithms.

Let T be a triangular segment of image containing N pixels with L gray levels that vary in the closed interval $(0,255)$. Let $F(i,j)$ be the gray value of the original image at pixel (i,j) and $G(i,j)$ be the predicted value using the linear interpolation of gray values at the triangle vertices.

3.2.1 Average Difference

Average difference (AD) [12] is defined as

$$AD = \frac{1}{N} \int \int |F(x,y) - G(x,y)| dxdy$$

In case of triangular segment of image T the AD is

$$AD = \frac{1}{N} \sum_{i,j \in T} |F(i,j) - G(i,j)| \tag{3.1}$$

AD as a basis for subdivision has desirable properties of uniqueness and simplicity. Also, every gray value in the triangular region contributes to the AD measure.

3.2.2 Entropy

Raw data do not necessarily represent information rate. The average self information rate is given by the entropy (H) [26] and is defined as

$$H = -\sum P(A_i) \log_x P(A_i)$$

where, A_i is a set of independent events, and $P(A_i)$ is the probability of the event A_i. For triangular segment of image T entropy is

$$H = -\sum_{i=0}^{L} P_i \log_2^{P_i}, i \in T \tag{3.2}$$

where P_i is the probability of the gray level i. This is called the zeroth-order entropy since no consideration is given to the fact that a given sample may have statistical dependence on its neighbors.

3.2.3 Normalized Mean Square Error

In general, it is difficult to examine the difference between original image gray value and predicted gray value on term-by-term basis. Therefore, average measures are used to summarize the information. The most often used is the average of the squared error measure. This is called the normalized mean square error [12] and is defined as

$$NMSE = \frac{\int \int (F(x,y) - G(x,y))^2 dxdy}{\int \int (F(x,y))^2 dxdy}$$

For triangular segment of image T normalized mean square error is

$$\text{NMSE} = \frac{\sum\limits_{i,j \in T} (F(i,j) - G(i,j))^2}{\sum\limits_{i,j \in T} (F(i,j))^2} \tag{3.3}$$

3.2.4 Fuzzy Compactness

The image can be interpreted as an array of fuzzy singletons [14, 27, 28]. Each pixel has a membership value depending upon its brightness relative to some level l, $l = 0, 1, 2 \ldots L - 1$ i.e. $X = \{\mu_x(X_{ij}) = \mu_{ij}/X_{ij}; i,j = 1, 2 \ldots m\}$ where $\mu_x(X_{ij})$; or $\mu_{ij}/X_{ij}(0 \le \mu_{ij} \le 1)$ denotes the grade of possessing some brightness property μ_{ij} by the (i,j)th pixel intensity X_{ij}. Rosenfeld [13, 16, 17, 29, 30] extended the concepts of digital picture geometry to fuzzy subsets and generalized some of the standard geometric properties and relationships among regions to fuzzy sets. Among the extensions of the various properties, we only discuss here the area, perimeter and compactness of fuzzy image subset, characterized by $\mu_x(X_{ij})$, which will be used in the following section for developing fuzzy compactness (FC) algorithm. In defining the above mentioned parameters we replace $\mu_x(X_{ij})$ by μ for simplicity.

The area of μ is defined as

$$a(\mu) = \int \mu$$

where the integral is taken over any region outside which $\mu = 0$. If μ is piecewise constant (e.g. in the case of a triangular segment of image T) the area is

$$a(\mu) = \sum \mu = \sum_i \sum_j \mu(i,j) \text{ with } i,j = 1, 2 \ldots m, \ i,j \in T \tag{3.4}$$

For the piecewise constant case the perimeter of μ is defined as

$$P(\mu) = \sum_{i,j} \sum_k |\mu_i - \mu_j| |A_{ijk}| \quad i,j = 1, 2 \ldots r, \ i < j; \ k = 1, 2 \ldots r_{ij.} \tag{3.5}$$

This is the weighted sum of the lengths of the arcs A_{ijk} along which the ith and jth regions having constant μ values μ_i and μ_j, respectively meet, weighted by the absolute difference of the values. In the case of an image, if we consider the pixels as the piecewise constant regions, then the perimeter of an image is defined by

$$P(\mu) = \sum_{i,j} |\mu(x_{i,j}) - \mu(x_{i,j+1})| + |\mu(x_{i,j} - \mu(x_{i+1,j})|$$

Fig. 3.1 Representation of adjacent pixels in the image

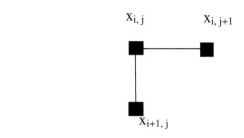

Fig. 3.2 Pictorial representation of membership function

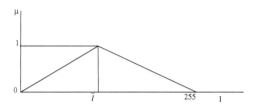

where $\mu(x_{i,\ j})$, $\mu(x_{i,\ j+1})$ and $\mu(x_{i+1,\ j})$ are the membership values of adjacent pixels. As shown in Fig. 3.1 only the east and south neighbors are considered and $i,j \in k$th triangle.

The compactness of μ is defined as

$$\text{Comp}(\mu) \;=\; a\;(\mu)/\,P^2(\mu) \tag{3.6}$$

For the purpose of image domain decomposition, we assign memberships to pixels belonging to triangular domain of the image as follows and shown in Fig. 3.2.

If $I = \bar{I}$ then $\mu = 1$
Else If $I < \bar{I}$ then $\mu = I/\bar{I}$
Else $\mu = (255 - I)/(255 - \bar{I})$
Endif.

where $\bar{I} = \frac{1}{n_k}\sum_{m=1}^{k} I_m$, $\bar{I}$ is the mean intensity of the kth triangle and n_k is the total number of pixels in kth triangle.

These membership values denote the similarities of the pixel brightness to the brightness of a typical prototype pixel in the region. The typical brightness value is taken as the arithmetic mean of all the pixels belonging to that region.

After the memberships are assigned, the FC of the region is computed using Eq. 3.6. The use of compactness rather than intensity deviation at a single pixel gives us an image compression algorithm, which is robust and requires less number of subdivisions. The decision to further sub divide a triangle region into smaller triangles is taken based on the value computed using Eq. 3.6 against the user specified quality parameter. The pseudo code of FC algorithm [23, 24] is given in Sect. 3.2.4.1.

3.2.4.1 Fuzzy BTTC Algorithm

//L is list of leaves with no processing

1. Set $L = NULL$;
   Set $T_1 = <(1,1)(1,m)(m,\ 1)>$, $T_2 = <(m,\ m)(m,\ 1)(1,m)>$.
2. Push T_1 and T_2 into stack.
3. Pop the Triangle T from stack.
   Let $P_1 = (x_1,\ y_1)$, $P_2 = (x_2,\ y_2)$, $P_3 = (x_3,\ y_3)$ be it's vertices.
   Set $C_1 = F(x_1,\ y_1)$, $C_2 = F(x_2,\ y_2)$, $C_3 = F(x_3,\ y_3)$.
4. Calculate the compactness of the triangle T using Eq. 3.6.
5. If compactness exceeds the quality factor (e) then goto step 7.
6. Set $P_{max} = (P_2 + P_3)/2$; Set $T_1 = <P_{max}\ P_3\ P_1>$; $T_2 = <P_{max}\ P_1\ P_2>$
   goto step 2.
7. Insert T into L.
8. If the stack is empty then stop, otherwise goto step 3.

Similarly for other algorithms based on quality measures listed in this section, AD, Entropy, and NMSE of the triangle are calculated using Eqs. 3.1–3.3 respectively and compared with quality factor (e). If these measures exceed the quality factor, the triangle is divided into two smaller triangles relative to the hypotenuse. Decoding is analogous to encoding, with the only difference being that the quality of the approximation need not be tested and linear interpolation will be used instead of compactness, AD, entropy and NMSE in step 4 of the algorithm.

3.2.5 Computing Time

Encoding algorithms using quality measures require a time proportional to an, where n is the number of pixels and 'a' expresses the average number of subdivisions per pixel. An upper bound for a is therefore $O(nlogn)$ yielding the worst case time $O(nlogn)$. In decompression the first and second steps are performed in $\theta(t)$ time, where t is the number of nodes in the tree. The remaining steps in the algorithms can be completed in $\theta(n)$ time. Since $t < n$, the time complexity for decompression is $\theta(n)$.

3.3 Experimental Results

To evaluate the performance of all the segmented BTTC methods several 8-bit 512×512 test images were used. All the partitioning methods discussed in Sect. 3.2 give consistently better performance than the BTTC on all test images we used. This section presents some results obtained on test images Lenna, Barbara, Cameraman, Baboon and World Trade Center (wtc) as shown in Fig. 3.3.

Fig. 3.3 Original test images Lenna, Barbara, Cameraman, Baboon and World Trade Center (wtc) from *top left*

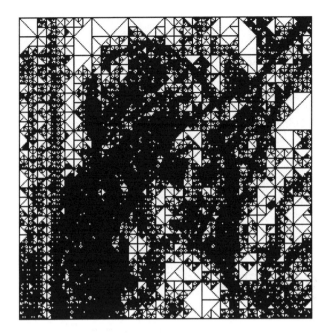

Fig. 3.4 Domain triangulation for image lenna using AD

Table 3.2 Distortion measures for the image lenna

Compression ratio	Peak signal to noise ratio				
	BTTC	AD	Entropy (H)	NMSE	FC
1.85	38.46	46.26	39.79	43.21	46.89
2.16	36.96	42.41	37.56	41.04	44.34
2.46	35.79	41.71	36.31	38.14	43.11
2.70	34.77	39.12	35.21	37.47	41.09
2.93	33.82	38.77	34.67	37.38	39.50
3.45	32.30	36.74	33.11	35.74	37.50
3.96	30.42	35.77	31.53	33.23	36.49
4.21	29.51	33.98	30.50	31.62	34.52

Figure 3.4 shows the domain partition of the test image Lenna using AD. Table 3.2 shows the distortion measures for test image Lenna for different partitioning methods. In Table 3.2 the first column lists the compression ratio and the remaining five columns gives the peak signal to noise ratio (PSNR) for BTTC, AD, Entropy, NMSE, and FC based partitioning methods, respectively. As shown in Fig. 3.5 by using all the partitioning techniques the quality of the reconstructed image significantly improves when compared to basic BTTC at similar compression ratios for all the test images shown in Fig. 3.3. FC gives better quality when compared to the other partitioning methods discussed in this chapter. From Figs. 3.5 and 3.6 it can be observed that as the compression ratio increases the

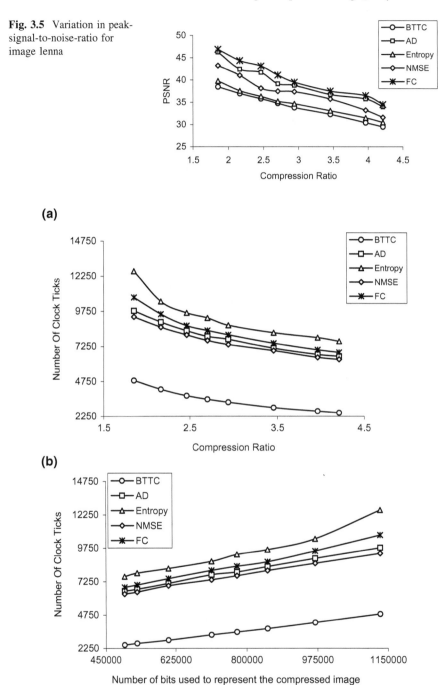

Fig. 3.5 Variation in peak-signal-to-noise-ratio for image lenna

(a)

(b)

Fig. 3.6   a, b Variation in number of clock ticks for image lenna

Table 3.3 Computing time statistics for the image lenna

Compression ratio	Compressed image (bits)	Number of clock ticks				
		BTTC	AD	Entropy (H)	NMSE	FC
1.85	1,130,564	4,828	9,781	12,609	9,360	10,734
2.16	968,772	4,187	8,984	10,450	8,625	9,546
2.46	851,047	3,735	8,375	9,640	8,078	8,729
2.70	776,118	3,484	7,968	9,288	7,688	8,399
2.93	713,403	3,265	7,772	8,768	7,390	8,088
3.45	606,798	2,875	7,125	8,234	6,953	7,479
3.96	529,223	2,625	6,683	7,888	6,469	7,002
4.21	497,910	2,500	6,547	7,625	6,328	6,823

PSNR value decreases and less number of clock ticks is required. At higher compression ratio the reconstructed image is more distorted, consequently PSNR value of the reconstructed image is less. Less number of triangles is formed at high compression ratio and less number of clock ticks is required to compress the image. Figure 3.6b shows that the number of bits required to represent the image increases and the number of clock ticks required to compress the image decreases. At lower compression ratios, number of clock ticks required is more; also more number of triangles are formed.

Table 3.3 shows the computing time statistics for the image Lenna. In Table 3.3 first column specifies the compression ratio, second column specifies the compressed image in bits and the following columns specify the time taken to compress the image using different partitioning methods. It can be seen from Fig. 3.6 that the computing time for AD, Entropy, NMSE, and FC are high when compared to BTTC. Comparative performance of the partitioning methods using test images Cameraman, wtc, Lenna, Barbara, and Baboon at the same compression ratio of 2.939 is shown in Fig. 3.7. The reconstructed images of Lenna using AD at compression ratios 1.85, 2.16, 2.46 and 2.70 are shown in Fig. 3.8. Subsampled Lenna image scaled by factor 4 and domain triangulation of subsampled Lenna using BTTC, AD, Entropy, NMSE and FC are shown in Fig. 3.9. It can be seen from Fig. 3.9 that the orientation of triangles are different in each partitioning method discussed in this chapter even with the number of triangles formed held constant.

From Fig. 3.10 it can be seen that the quality of the reconstructed image using JPEG2000 is high compared to JPEG and BTTC at the same compression ratio. The time taken to compress the given image using JPEG2000 is also high compared to JPEG and BTTC as shown in Fig. 3.11. The histogram and 3D surface of original Lenna image is given in Figs. 3.12 and 3.13 respectively. The histograms of the reconstructed image using BTTC, JPEG and JPEG2000 are shown in Figs. 3.14, 3.15 and 3.16 at same CPU time i.e. 705 clock ticks. The error images of Lenna scaled by factor 10 using BTTC, JPEG and JPEG2000 are given in Fig. 3.17 at same number of clock ticks. From Fig. 3.17 it can be observed that distortion in the reconstructed image using BTTC is less when compared to JPEG

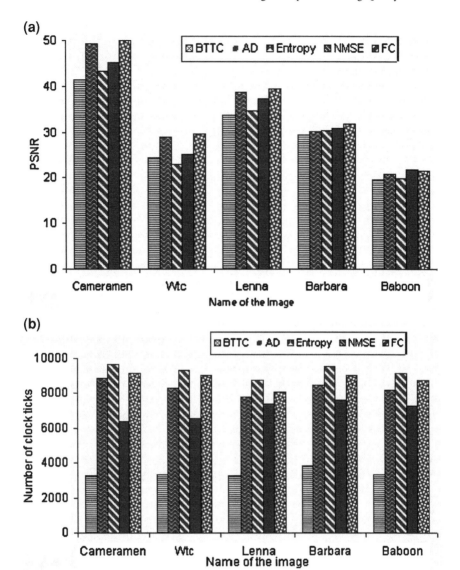

Fig. 3.7 Comparative results of *BTTC*, *AD*, *Entropy*, *NMSE* and *FC* using test images *Cameraman*, *Wtc*, *Lenna*, *Barbara*, And *Baboon* at similar compression ratio 2.939 **a** variation in PSNR and **b** variation in number of clock ticks

Fig. 3.8 Reconstructed lenna images using AD at compression ratios 1.85, 2.16, 2.46 and 2.70 from *top left*

and JPEG2000 at same number of clock ticks. By observing Figs. 3.11, 3.12, 3.13, 3.14, 3.15, 3.16, and 3.17 we find that the BTTC algorithm is faster than the state of art techniques i.e. JPEG and JPEG2000. 3D surface of the reconstructed image Lenna at 705 clock ticks using BTTC, JPEG, JPEG2000 is shown in Fig. 3.18.

3.4 Conclusions

In this chapter, we have discussed the idea of using different image quality measures as a basis of domain decomposition based image compression. This idea has resulted in improvement of the recently reported BTTC algorithm. BTTC takes a decision to subdivide based on the error at a single pixel. On the other hand, the partitioning methods discussed in this chapter take a subdivision decision based on well-established quality measures like AD, Entropy, NMSE and FC of the entire parent triangle. AD as a basis for subdivision has desirable properties of uniqueness and simplicity. Every gray value in the triangular region contributes to the AD

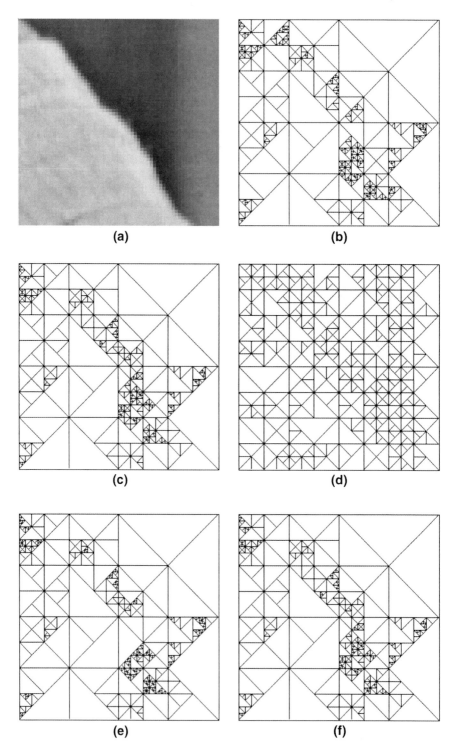

Fig. 3.9 Distribution of triangulation with different quality factors: **a** Subsampled Lenna image scaled by factor 4 and domain triangulation of subsampled Lenna using **b** BTTC, **c** AD, **d** Entropy, **e** NMSE, **f** FC at same number of triangles i.e. 380

Fig. 3.10 Variation in peak-
signal-to-noise-ratio for
image Lenna

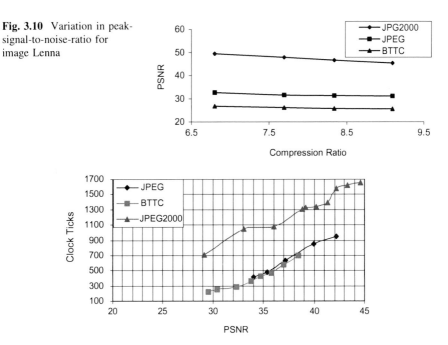

Fig. 3.11 Variation in number of clock ticks for image Lenna

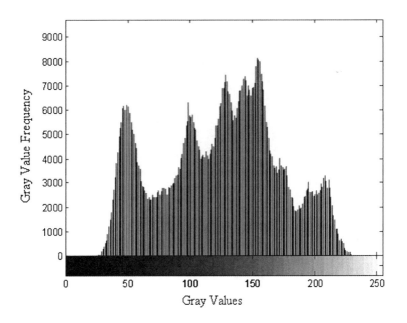

Fig. 3.12 Histogram of original Lenna image

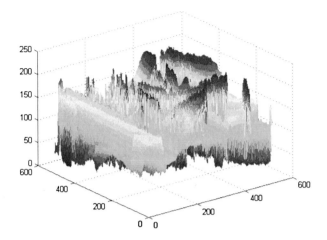

Fig. 3.13 3D surface representation of the original Lenna

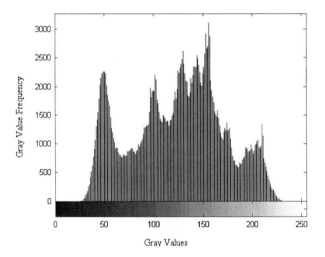

Fig. 3.14 Histogram of reconstructed Lenna image using BTTC at 705 clock ticks

measure. Entropy gives the self-information rate of the triangle. NMSE summarizes the information of the parent triangle. FC offers the advantages of reduced triangulation and better noise immunity. Since BTTC takes a hard decision to subdivide based on the maximum error at a single pixel, noisy pixels force many unnecessary subdivisions. On the other hand, FC takes a subdivision decision based on FC of the entire parent triangle, thereby avoiding unnecessary subdivisions due to outliers. Use of quality measures distributes the triangles rationally by

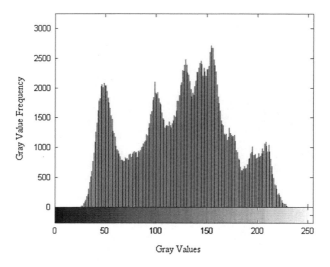

Fig. 3.15 Histogram of reconstructed Lenna image using JPEG at 705 clock ticks

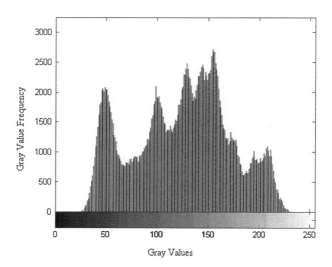

Fig. 3.16 Histogram of reconstructed Lenna image using JPEG2000 at 705 clock ticks

placing more number of triangles near interesting features like edges. Further the quality of reconstructed image is significantly better than BTTC for comparable compression ratios. FC gives by far the best results and has additional desirable

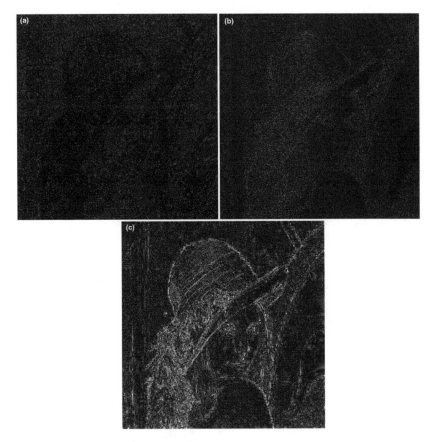

Fig. 3.17 **a** Error image Lenna scaled by factor 10 using *BTTC* at 705 clock ticks. **b** Error image lenna scaled by factor 10 using *JPEG* at 705 clock ticks. **c** Error image Lenna scaled by factor 10 using *JPEG2000* at 705 clock ticks

property of noise immunity. The new methods have the same computational complexity as the original version of BTTC. All these encoding techniques have faster execution time than JPEG and JPEG2000.

In this chapter, we have proposed image compression algorithms using quality measures and compared with other lossy image compression techniques. In the next chapter we discuss parallel implementation of these algorithms.

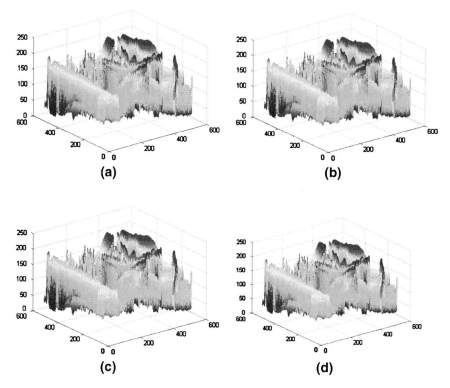

Fig. 3.18 3D surface representation of **a** original Lenna image and reconstructed of Lenna at 705 clock ticks using **b** BTTC, **c** JPEG and **d** JPEG2000

References

1. Wu X, Fang Y (1995) A segmentation-based predictive multiresolution image coder. IEEE Trans Image Process 4:34–47
2. Strobach P (1989) Image coding based on quadtree-structured recursive least squares approximation. Proc IEEE ICAASP 89:1961–1964
3. Wu X (1992) Image coding by adaptive tree-structured segmentation. IEEE Trans Inform Theory 38(6):1755–1767
4. Jiang W, Bruton L (1998) Lossless color image compression using chromatic correlation. In: IEEE proceedings of data compression conference
5. Da Silva VC, De Carvalho JM (2000) Image compression via TRITREE decomposition. In: Proceedings of the XIII Brazilian symposium on computer graphics and image processing (SIBGRAPI)
6. Li X, Knipe J, Cheng H (1997) Image compression and encryption using tree structures. Pattern Recognit Lett 18:1253–1259
7. Vitulano S, Di Ruberto C, Nappi M (1997) Different methods to segment biomedical images. Pattern Recognit Lett 18:1125–1131
8. Lundmark A, Wadstromer N, Li H (2001) Hierarchical subsampling giving fractal regions. IEEE Trans Image Process 4(1):167–173

 9. Biswas S, Pal NR (2000) On hierarchical segmentation for image compression. Pattern Recognit Lett 21:131–144
10. Eckert MP, Bradley AP (1998) Perceptual quality metrics applied to still image compression. Signal Process 70:177–200
11. Davoine F, Antonini M, Chassery JM, Barlaud M (1996) Fractal image compression based on delaunay triangulation and vector quantization. IEEE Trans Image Process 5(2):338–346
12. Eskicioglu AM, Fisher PS (1995) Image quality measures and their performance. IEEE Trans Commun 43(12):2959–2965
13. Rosenfeld A (1984) The fuzzy geometry of image subsets. Pattern Recognit Lett 2:311–317
14. Pal SK, Rosenfeld A (1988) Image enhancement and thresholding by optimization of fuzzy compactness. Pattern Recognit Lett 7:77–86
15. Pal SK (1989) Fuzzy skeletanization of an image. Pattern Recognit Lett 10:17–23
16. Rosenfeld A (1979) Fuzzy digital topology. Inform Control 40:76–87
17. Rosenfeld A (1983) On connectivity properties of gray scale pictures. Pattern Recognit 16:47–50
18. Hirota K, Pedryez W (2002) Data compression with fuzzy relational equations. Fuzzy Sets Syst 126:325–335
19. Tizhoosh HR, Krell G, Michaelis G (1997) On fuzzy enhancement of megavoltage images in radiation therapy. In: IEEE conference on fuzzy systems, FUZZ-IEEE'97, vol 3. Barcelona, Spain, pp 1399–1404
20. Tizhoosh HR, Michaelis B (1999) Subjectivity, psychology and fuzzy techniques: a new approach to image enhancement. In: Proceedings of 18th international conference of NAFIPS'99, New York, pp 522–526
21. Nobuhara H, Pedrycz W, Harota K (2000) Fast solving method of fuzzy relational equation and its application to lossy image compression/reconstruction. IEEE Trans Fuzzy Sys 8(3): 325–334
22. Sinha D, Sinha P, Dougherty ER, Batman S (1997) Design and analysis of fuzzy morphological algorithms for image processing. IEEE Trans Fuzzy Syst 5:570–584
23. Prasad MVNK, Mishra VN, Shukla KK (2003) Space partitioning based image compression using quality measures. Applied soft computing, vol. 3. Elsevier Science, Amsterdam, pp. 273–282
24. Prasad MVNK, Shukla KK, Mukherjee RN (2002) Implementation of BTTC image compression Algorithm Using Fuzzy Technique, AFSS2002. In: Proceedings of the international conference on fuzzy systems, Calcutta, pp 375–381, February 2002, ISBN 3-540-43150-0
25. Distasi R, Nappi M, Vitulano S (1997) Image compression by B-tree triangular coding. IEEE Trans Commun 45(9):1095–1100
26. Jain AK (1981) Image data compression: a review. Proc IEEE 69(3):349–389
27. Pal SK, Ghosh A (1990) Index of area coverage of fuzzy image subsets and extraction. Pattern Recognit Lett 11:831–841
28. Pal SankarK, Ghosh Ashish (1992) Fuzzy geometry in image analysis. Fuzzy Sets Syst 48:22–40
29. Rosenfeld A, Haber S (1985) The perimeter of fuzzy set. Pattern Recognit 18:125–130
30. Rosenfeld A (1984) The diameter of fuzzy set. Fuzzy Sets Systems 13:241–246

Chapter 4
Parallel Image Compression Algorithms

Abstract This Chapter presents parallel version of domain decomposition algorithms on different architectures like Concurrent Read Exclusive Write (CREW) Parallel Random Access Machine (PRAM), Hypercube, 2D Mesh, and Sparse Mesh. Time complexities of these algorithms are also derived. Implementation of the domain decomposition algorithm on Parallel Virtual Machine (PVM) environment using Master–slave paradigm has been described. Parallel program profiles and speed up measurements are given.

Keywords Domain decomposition · Parallel algorithms · PRAM · Hypercube · Mesh · PVM · Complexity

This Chapter presents algorithms for parallel implementation of domain decomposition based image compression on four models, viz., (i) Concurrent Read Exclusive Write (CREW) Parallel Random Access Machine (PRAM), (ii) Hypercube, (iii) 2D Mesh, and (iv) Sparse mesh. The respective time complexities of these parallel algorithms are: $O(O(\frac{n}{p}log(\frac{n}{p})))$, $O(\frac{n}{p}(log(\frac{n}{p}) + log\,p))$, $O(\frac{n}{p}(log(\frac{n}{p}) + log\sqrt{p}))$ and $O(\frac{n}{p}(log(\frac{n}{p}) + log\,p))$ for encoding, where n is total number of pixels in the image and p is number of processors. Decomposition based image compression algorithm implementation on Parallel Virtual Machine (PVM) is also investigated.

4.1 Parallel Domain Decomposition

Several researchers have investigated parallel data compression in the recent past [1–5]. The general idea is that the original image is first equally divided into blocks of possibly large size and the characteristics of each block are determined by looking into the statistics of the pixel gray values. Blocks that fail to pass the test are regarded as "rough blocks" and are further spilt into smaller blocks

K. K. Shukla and M. V. Prasad, *Lossy Image Compression*,
SpringerBriefs in Computer Science, DOI: 10.1007/978-1-4471-2218-0_4,
© K. K. Shukla 2011

(sub blocks). The process is carried out recursively until the sub blocks are very smooth and then these blocks are encoded. In the parallel algorithms presented in this book, we divide the image into triangles such that there is no data dependency among the triangles [6–8], [1–4], [9–21].

Sibeyn [9] introduced sparse mesh architecture, which has processing elements on the diagonal of a two-dimensional grid and is a cost effective distributed memory architecture. Various fundamental problems (routing, sorting, list ranking) have been analyzed in the literature proving that the sparse meshes have great potential for parallel computation. Cook and Delp [7] proposed parallel implementation of JPEG still image compression standard on MasPar MP-1, a massively parallel SIMD computer. They proposed a novel byte oriented algorithm used to efficiently output compressed data from the parallel system. Lee and Tanaka [11] describe a general-purpose parallel algorithm for image segmentation that does not require any prior knowledge about image properties. The algorithm is based on adaptive mesh generation scheme and provides binary tree structured split-and-merge mechanism to search and localize boundaries along discontinuities. It then adapts the partition of image to those detected discontinuities. The algorithm does not depend upon the order of processing or the starting point, which is an important issue in parallel algorithms. It maintains one pixel wide overlapping boundary between process blocks. By adopting smoothness-based local feature as homogeneity criteria, consistencies are maintained without the overhead of communication between adjacent process blocks. Efficient hierarchical step-wise mechanism in merging target evaluation makes merge process very simple and efficient.

Lee et al. [12] proposed a parallel architecture for quad tree based fractal image coding. The architecture is capable of performing the fractal image coding based on quad tree partitioning without any external memory for the fixed domain pool. A large domain block always consists of smaller blocks. The calculations of distortion are performed by the summation of the distortions for the maximum depth domain pool, which is extracted from the smallest range blocks of the neighboring processors. A fast comparison module has also been proposed for this architecture. This module can efficiently compute the distortions between range blocks and their eight isometric transformations by one full rotation around the center.

Jacson and Blom [13] proposed a parallel fractal image compression algorithm for hypercube multiprocessors using Master–slave paradigm. Their algorithm gives linear speedup when additional processing nodes are utilized. Miguet and Pierson [14] introduced two parallel heuristics that computes the suboptimal partitions with better complexity than the best-known algorithms that computes optimal partitions and gave theoretical bounds on the quality of these heuristics. This Chapter presents four new parallel image compression algorithms for PRAM, Hypercube, 2D mesh and Sparse mesh models.

4.2 Coding Scheme

The coding scheme described in this Chapter is based on parallel domain decomposition. The decomposition scheme involves triangulating the domain recursively as discussed in Sect. 2.3.1. Linear interpolation has been chosen since it gives acceptable quality of the reconstructed image, and has low computational cost as compared to other methods like Splines or Bezier curves. The interpolation performed by BTTC requires only four floating-point multiplications and one floating-point division per pixel as discussed in Sect. 2.3.1 as a result, it runs much faster than the standard techniques based on transforms.

4.2.1 Implementation on CREW PRAM Model

A PRAM model consists of a control unit, a global memory, and an unbounded set of processors. During computation, a processor may activate another processor and the computation terminates when the last processor halts. PRAM algorithms have two phases. In the first phase, a sufficient number of processors are activated and in the second phase, these activated processors perform computation in parallel [1].

For data distribution, consider any region in the image bound by a right-angled isosceles triangle $V_1V_2V_3$ as shown in Fig. 4.1. Draw lines parallel to the base of the triangle such that the triangle is split into z disjoint regions of equal area, where z is a variable denoting the number of processors assigned to the triangle. This results in one triangular area and $z-1$ trapezoidal areas as shown in Fig. 4.1b. It is straightforward to show that equal area subdivisions are specified by:

$$
\begin{aligned}
a_i &= \left\lceil (x_2(\sqrt{n/i} - 1) + x_1)/\sqrt{n/i} \right\rceil \ where\ i = 1\ to\ n - 1 \\
b_i &= \left\lceil (y_2(\sqrt{n/i} - 1) + y_1)/\sqrt{n/i} \right\rceil \\
c_i &= \left\lceil (x_2(\sqrt{n/i} - 1) + x_3)/\sqrt{n/i} \right\rceil \\
d_i &= \left\lceil (y_2(\sqrt{n/i} - 1) + y_3)/\sqrt{n/i} \right\rceil
\end{aligned}
\tag{4.1}
$$

Now the gray values corresponding to these subdivisions are distributed among z processors so that initially every processor is assigned equal workload. If any processor find that the predicted gray value using linear interpolation is greater than the threshold for any pixel in that region, all processors are stopped and the triangle is divided into two smaller triangles as shown in Fig. 4.1c. This process is repeated for all triangles. If the sub division procedure is iterated indefinitely, we eventually obtain a minimal triangle comprising of only three pixels, namely their vertices. The algorithm is formally given in Sect. 4.2.1.1.

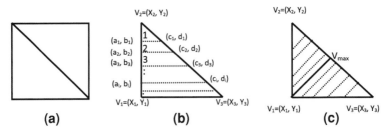

Fig. 4.1 (a) The image is divided into two triangles, (b)Dividing the triangle into z regions of equal area shown by *dotted lines* (c) One triangle is split into two smaller triangles shown by *solid line* and each triangle is divided into z regions of equal area shown by *dotted lines*

4.2.1.1 PRAM Algorithm

// p is number of processors
// L is list of leaves with no further processing requirements
//m is the size of the image
Global i, L

1. Set $L = NULL$.
2. Set $T_1 = ((1, 1)(1, m)(m, 1))$, $T_2 = ((m, m)(m, 1)(1, m))$ and assign $\lceil p/2 \rceil$ and $\lfloor p/2 \rfloor$ processors respectively to each of the two triangle.
3. For $j = 1$ to $\lceil log\, p \rceil$

   Pram();

4. // After assigning $\lfloor n/p \rfloor$ pixels to each processor

   For all p_i $1 \leq i \leq p$
       Bttc (); // call Bttc subprogram
   Endfor.
   Step 2 of the PRAM algorithm will divide the original image into two triangles. In step 3 the triangles are further subdivided into smaller triangles and assign number of processors to each triangle. After assigning $\lfloor n/p \rfloor$ pixels to each processor, sequential BTTC algorithm will be performed.
   //Pram subprogram
   Pram()
   //z is the number of processors assigned to each triangle
   Local z;
   Begin
   For all p_j $1 \leq j \leq p$

1. If ($\lfloor z/2 \rfloor == 0$)

   BTTC();
   Endif.

2. Let $V_1 = (x_1, y_1)$, $V_2 = (x_2, y_2)$, $V_3 = (x_3, y_3)$ be vertices of T

Set $C_1 = F(x_1, y_1)$; $C_2 = F(x_2, y_2)$; $C_3 = F(x_3, y_3)$;
For all p_z $1 \leq z \leq p$

   (a) Divide T into z regions of equal area and assign each to a processor as shown in Fig. 4.1(a) & 4.1(b).

   (b) For each pixel $(x, y) \in T$, calculate $G(x, y)$ using Eq. (2.3), (2.4) and (2.5); if the Eq. (2.8) is satisfied for each point, then go to step (d). If any processor finds Eq. (2.8) does not hold stop all z processors

   (c) // Divide T into two triangles by drawing its height relative to

//hypotenuse

Set $V_{max} = (V_2 + V_3)/2$
Set $T_1 = (V_{max}, V_1, V_2)$, $T_2 = (V_{max}, V_3, V_1)$ and assign $\lceil z/2 \rceil$, $\lfloor z/2 \rfloor$ processors respectively to each triangle.

   (d) Insert T into L_i
   Endfor.
Endfor.
End.

In step 1 of the Pram subprogram, if the number of processors assigned to the triangle is equal to 1, the sequential BTTC algorithm is executed, otherwise the triangle is divided into a number of regions of equal area as stated in step 2(a). Each region is assigned to one of the processors to calculate the prediction error. If any processor finds that the error is greater than the user defined threshold, the triangle is divided into two smaller triangles and processors are assigned to each triangle as shown in Fig. 4.1c. In case the error for all the pixels in a triangle is less than the threshold, it is inserted into the list L.

// Bttc subprogram
Bttc ()
Begin

   1. Let $V_1 = (x_1, y_1)$, $V_2 = (x_2, y_2)$ $V_3 = (x_3, y_3)$ be vertices of T

      Set $C_1 = F(x_1, y_1)$; $C_2 = F(x_2, y_2)$; $C_3 = F(x_3, y_3)$

   2. For each pixel $(x, y) \in T$, calculate $G(x, y)$ using Eq. (2.3), (2.4) and (2.5); if the Eq. (2.8) is satisfied for each point, then go to step 4.

   3. // Divide T into two smaller triangles by drawing its height relative to // hypotenuse

      Set $V_{max} = (V_2 + V_3)/2$
      Set $T_1 = (V_{max}, V_1, V_2)$, $T_2 = (V_{max}, V_3, V_1)$
      Push T_1 and T_2 into the stack.
      Pop T from the stack go to step 2.

   4. Insert T into L stop processor p_i.
   5. If stack is empty then stop processor P_i, otherwise pop T and go to step 2.

End.

BTTC subprogram is same as sequential BTTC algorithm discussed in Chap. 2. In PRAM algorithm since the vertex gray values of a triangle is shared by more than one processors, concurrent read is required. While writing, only one processor will write in the list (L) at any given time, hence exclusive write is necessary. Therefore, the CREW model is used in our PRAM algorithm.

4.2.1.2 Computing Time

In the PRAM algorithm, each processor processes $\frac{n}{p}$ pixels and number of subdivisions per pixel is $O(log(\frac{n}{p}))$. Hence, the time complexity of PRAM algorithm for coding is $O(\frac{n}{p} log(\frac{n}{p}))$ using p processors.

The cost [15] of the PRAM algorithm = parallel running time × number of processors

$$= O\left(\frac{n}{p} log\left(\frac{n}{p}\right)\right) \, p$$

$$= O\left(n \, log\left(\frac{n}{p}\right)\right)$$

Lower bound of sequential algorithm is Ω $(n \, log \, n)$ and is greater than the cost of the parallel algorithm. Hence, the CREW PRAM algorithm is cost optimal.

4.2.2 Implementation on Hypercube Model

The hypercube architecture consists of 2^k processing nodes forming a k-dimensional hypercube. The nodes are labeled $0,1,....,2^{k-1}$. In this model there is no shared memory and processors interact by passing messages to each other. The algorithm for hypercube model is given in Sect. 4.2.2.1. In step 1 of the algorithm the image is divided into two right-angled triangles that are assigned to one processor each. In step 2 each processor calculates prediction error using (2.7) for each pixel and if error exceeds threshold value, the triangle is divided into two triangles along its height relative to the hypotenuse and one of the new triangles is assigned to the another processor in the hypercube as shown in Fig. 4.2. This process is carried out in all processors in parallel. In step 3, after assigning the $\lfloor n/p \rfloor$ pixels to each processor sequential BTTC algorithm is executed concurrently in all the processors [1].

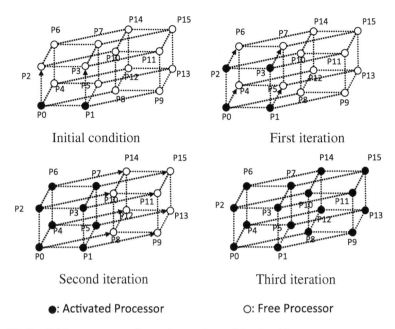

Fig. 4.2 Parallel image compression on hypercube model using 16 processors

4.2.2.1 Hypercube Algorithm

// p is the number of processors
//m is the size of the given image
Global i, L

1. Set $L = NULL$.

   Set $T_1 = ((1, 1)(1, m)(m, 1))$, $T_2 = ((m, m)(m, 1)(1, m))$ and assign to p_0, p_1 processors respectively.

2. For $j = 1$ to $\log p$-1

       For all p_i $0 \le i \le p$-1
        If $i < 2^j$
           Cube(); // Call Cube subprogram
        Endif
       Endfor
     Endfor

3. // After assigning $\lfloor n/p \rfloor$ pixels to each processor

       For all p_i $1 \le i \le p$
        Bttc (); // Call Bttc subprogram
       Endfor.
   // Cube subprogram

Cube()
// L is the list of leaves with no further processing requirements
Begin

1. Let $V_1 = (x_1, y_1)$, $V_2 = (x_2, y_2)$ $V_3 = (x_3, y_3)$ be vertices of triangle T

   Set $C_1 = F(x_1, y_1)$; $C_2 = F(x_2, y_2)$; $C_3 = F(x_3, y_3)$;

2. For each pixel $(x, y) \in T$, calculate $G(x, y)$ using Eq. (2.3), (2.4) and (2.5);

   if the Eq. (2.8) is satisfied for each point, then go to step 4.

3. // Divide T into two smaller triangles by drawing its height relative to

   //hypotenuse

   Set $V_{max} = (V_2 + V_3)/2$
   Set $T_1 = (V_{max}, V_1, V_2)$, $T_2 = (V_{max}, V_3, V_1)$ and assign to p_i, p_{i+2^j} processors as shown in Fig.4.2.

4. Insert T into L.

End.

4.2.2.2 Computing Time

Each node processes $\frac{n}{p}$ pixels to perform compression and in the worst case, the processor performs $O(\frac{n}{p} \log p)$ communication steps. Hence, the time complexity of Hypercube BTTC algorithm is $O(\frac{n}{p}(\log(\frac{n}{p}) + \log p))$ or $O(\frac{n}{p}(\log(\frac{n}{p}) + k))$ for encoding where k is the dimension of the Hypercube.

4.2.3 Implementation on 2D Mesh Model

A 2D mesh consists of p processors that are organized in a $\sqrt{p} X \sqrt{p}$ grid where $\sqrt{p}$ is the size of the mesh. In this model also, there is no shared memory and the processors interact by passing the messages between them. The algorithm for 2D mesh model is given in Sect. 4.2.3.1. In step 1 of the algorithm the image is divided into two right-angled triangles and assigned to one processor each. In step 2 and 3 each processor calculates error using (2.7) for each pixel and if the error exceeds a threshold value, the triangle is divided into two triangles along its height relative to the hypotenuse and one of the new triangles is assigned to another processor in the mesh as shown in Fig. 4.3. Step 2 assigns the pixels to the neighboring processor in the same column and step 3 assigns the pixels to the neighboring processor in the neighboring column as shown in Fig. 4.3. This process is carried out in all processors in parallel. In step 4 after assigning the $\lfloor n/p \rfloor$ pixels to each processor sequential BTTC algorithm is executed in all the processors [1].

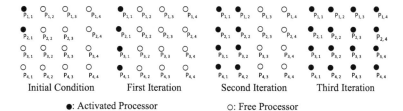

Fig. 4.3 Image Compression being performed on 16 Processors organized in a 2D mesh

4.2.3.1 2D Mesh Algorithm

// p is the number of processors
// S is the mesh size i.e. $\sqrt{p}$ (Integer power of two)
//m is the size of the given image
// a is a flag
Global i, L, a

1. Set $L = NULL$.

   Set $T_1 = ((1, 1)(1, m)(m, 1))$, $T_2 = ((m, m)(m, 1)(1, m))$ and assign to $p_{1, 1}, p_{1, 2}$ processors respectively.

2. For $z = 2$ to S step $2z$

      For all $p_{i, 1}$ $1 \leq i \leq z$
         Mesh (4.1); // Call mesh subprogram
      Endfor
   Endfor

3. For $z = 1$ to S step $2i$

      For all $p_{j, i}$ $1 \leq j \leq S, 1 \leq i \leq z$,
         Mesh (0); //Call mesh subprogram
      Endfor
   Endfor

4. // After assigning $\lfloor n/p \rfloor$ pixels to each processor

   For all p_i $1 \leq i \leq p$
   Bttc (); // Call Bttc subprogram
   Endfor
// Mesh subprogram
Mesh (a)
// L is list of leaves with no further processing requirements
Begin

1. Let $V_1 = (x_1, y_1), V_2 = (x_2, y_2)$ $V_3 = (x_3, y_3)$ be vertices of T

Set $C_1 = F(x_1, y_1)$; $C_2 = F(x_2, y_2)$; $C_3 = F(x_3, y_3)$;

2. For each pixel $(x, y) \in T$, calculate $G(x, y)$ using Eq. (2.3), (2.4) and (2.5);

   if the Eq. (2.8) is satisfied for each point, then go to step 4.

3. // Divide T into two smaller triangles by drawing its height relative to

   // the hypotenuse
   Set $V_{max} = (V_2 + V_3)/2$
   Set $T_1 = (V_{max}, V_1, V_2)$, $T_2 = (V_{max}, V_3, V_1)$
   If (flag) assign to $p_{i, 1}$, $p_{i+z, 1}$ processors as shown in Fig. 4.3.
   Else assign to $p_{j, i}$, $p_{j, i+z}$ processors

4. Insert T into L.

End.

4.2.3.2 Computing Time

The total number of communication steps to get the pixels to the last column of processors must be at least $O(\frac{n}{p} log \sqrt{p})$. Hence, the time complexity of Mesh BTTC algorithm is $O(\frac{n}{p}(log(\frac{n}{p}) + log \sqrt{p}))$ for encoding.

4.2.4 Implementation on Sparse Mesh

A sparse mesh with p processors consists of a two-dimensional $p \times p$ grid of buses, with processors connected at the diagonal. The horizontal buses are called row-buses; the vertical buses are called column-buses. Processors p_i, $1 \le i \le p$, can send data along the ith row-bus and receive data from the jth column-bus. In one step, p_i can send data to an arbitrary p_j. The data first travels along the ith row-bus position (i, j) and then turns into jth column-bus. The sparse mesh algorithm is given in Sect. 4.2.4.1. In step 2 each processor calculates error using (2.7) for each pixel and if the error exceeds the threshold value, the triangle is divided into two triangles along its height relative to the hypotenuse and one triangle will be assigned to the another processor in the sparse mesh as shown in Fig. 4.4. This process is carried out in all the processors in parallel. In step 3 after assigning the $\lfloor n/p \rfloor$ pixels to each processor, the sequential BTTC algorithm is executed in all processors [1].

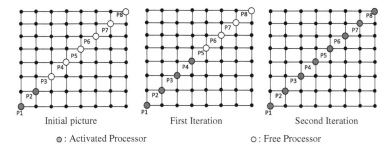

: Activated Processor   o : Free Processor

Fig. 4.4 Image Compression being performed on eight Processors organized as a sparse mesh

4.2.4.1 Sparse Mesh Algorithm

// p is number of processors
//m is the size of the image
Global i, L

1. Set $T_1 = ((1, 1)(1, m)(m, 1))$, $T_2 = ((m, m)(m, 1)(1, m))$ and assign to p_0, p_1 processors respectively.
2. For $j = 2$ to $\lceil log\, p \rceil$
    $z = p\text{-}2j;$
    If $(j == \lceil log\, p \rceil \&38; \&38; z! = 0)$
        For all p_i $1 \le i \le z$
          Sparse(); // Call sparse subprogram
        Endfor
    Else
        For all p_i $1 \le i \le p$
          Sparse(); // Call sparse subprogram
        Endfor
    Endif
  Endfor
Endfor

3. // After assigning $\lfloor n/p \rfloor$ pixels to each processor

  For all p_i $1 \le i \le p$
    Bttc (); // Call Bttc subprogram
  Endfor.
// Sparse subprogram
Sparse()
// L is list of leaves with no further processing requirements
Begin

1. Let $V_1 = (x_1, y_1)$, $V_2 = (x_2, y_2)$ $V_3 = (x_3, y_3)$ be vertices of T

  Set $C_1 = F(x_1, y_1)$; $C_2 = F(x_2, y_2)$; $C_3 = F(x_3, y_3)$

2. For each pixel $(x, y) \in T$, calculate $G(x, y)$ using Eq. (2.3), (2.4) and (2.5);

if the Eq. (2.8) is satisfied for each point, then go to step 4.

3. // Divide T into two smaller triangles by drawing its height relative to //the hypotenuse

Set $V_{max} = (V_2 + V_3)/2$
Set $T_1 = (V_{max}, V_1, V_2)$, $T_2 = (V_{max}, V_3, V_1)$ and assign to p_i, p_{i+j} processors as shown in Fig.4.4.

4. Insert T into L.
End.

4.2.4.2 Computing Time

Each processing element processes $\frac{n}{p}$ pixels. In the worst case, a processor must perform $O(\frac{n}{p} log p)$ communication steps. Hence, the time complexity of the sparse mesh BTTC algorithm is $O(\frac{n}{p}(log(\frac{n}{p}) + log p))$ for encoding with p processors.

4.2.5 Implementation on PVM

Increased computational size and time required for the solution of new scientific and engineering problems combined with the high cost of supercomputers has led to the need for fast but cost effective computing. One solution that makes use of available resources and reduces cost is the parallel utilization of networked heterogeneous computers. One software system currently available for this purpose is the PVM [2].

PVM is an integrated set of software tools and libraries that emulates a general-purpose, flexible, heterogeneous concurrent computing framework on interconnected computers of varied architecture. The overall objective of the PVM system is to enable a collection of computers to be used cooperatively for concurrent or parallel computation. Briefly, the principles upon which PVM is based include the following [16]:

1. *User-configured host pool* The application's computational tasks execute on a set of machines that are selected by the user for a given run of the PVM program. Both single-CPU machines and multiprocessors may be part of the host pool. Adding and deleting machines during operation may alter the host pool.

2. *Translucent access to hardware* Application programs either may view the hardware environment as an attributeless collection of virtual processing elements or may choose to exploit the capabilities of specific machines in the host pool by scheduling certain computational tasks on the most appropriate computers.

3. *Process-based computation* The unit of parallelism in PVM is a task (often but not always a Unix process), an independent sequential thread of control that alternates between communication and computation. No process-to-processor mapping is implied or enforced by PVM; in particular, multiple tasks may execute on a single processor.
4. *Explicit message-passing model* Collections of computational tasks, each performing a part of an application's workload, cooperate by explicitly sending and receiving messages to one another. Message size is limited only by the amount of available memory.
5. *Heterogeneity support* The PVM system supports heterogeneity in terms of machines, networks, and applications. With regard to message passing, PVM permits messages containing more than one data type that can be exchanged between machines having different data representations.
6. *Multiprocessor support* PVM uses the native message passing facilities on multiprocessors to take advantage of the underlying hardware.

The PVM computing model is based on the notion that an application consists of several tasks. Each task is responsible for a part of the application's computational workload. Sometimes an application is parallelized along its functions; that is, each task performs a different function, for example input problem setup, solution, output, and display. This decomposition is often called functional parallelism. A more common method of parallelizing an application is called data parallelism. In this method, all the tasks are the same, but each one only knows and solves a small part of the data. This is also referred to as the SPMD (single-program multiple-data) model of computing. PVM supports either or a mixture of these methods. Depending on their functions, tasks may execute in parallel and may need to synchronize or exchange data, although this is not always the case. A diagram of the PVM computing model is shown in Fig. 4.5 and an architectural view of the PVM system, highlighting the heterogeneity of the computing platforms supported by PVM, is shown in Fig. 4.6.

Parallel computing may be approached from three fundamental viewpoints, based on the organization of the computing tasks. The models are (i) Crowd Computation, (ii) Tree Computation and (iii) Hybrid Computation. The Crowd paradigm can be further subdivided into two categories: (1) Master–slave model and (2) Node-only model.

The master–slave (or host-node) model uses a separate "control" program (the master) for process spawning, initialization, collection and display of results. The slave programs perform the actual computation involved; they are assigned their workloads by the master or perform the allocations themselves.

The two general paradigms used in distributed system for load allocation are (i) Data decomposition and (ii) Function decomposition. In data decomposition a controlling process sends individual data subsets to each process. PVM has an in-built mechanism for load balancing which may be categorized as a coarse gained approach to load balancing. Before spawning any new process, PVM checks the

Fig. 4.5 PVM computing
model

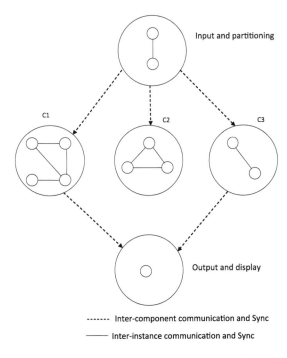

utilization of all the machines available to the virtual machine and the master
spawns the new process on the one that is least utilized.

Master–slave model and data decomposition are used in implementing the
BTTC image compression algorithm on PVM. Initially, the master processor
divides the image into k triangles, where k is an integer greater than one. p
processors are available to compress the image. Master processor allocates the
tasks to slaves using in-built load balancing mechanism in PVM. After completion
of data decomposition, master processor sends the corresponding vertices of the
triangles (individual data subsets) to each slave processor. The slave processor
compresses the subset data and the compressed data is transmitted to the master.
The master processor collects the compressed image data from all the slave processors and writes into the output file. The following PVM library functions are
used to implement the BTTC algorithm on PVM and the pseudo code of the master
and slave algorithms are shown in Sects. 4.2.5.1 and 4.2.5.2 respectively.

1. *pvm_mytid()* The routine enrolls the process into PVM on its first call and
   generates a unique task identifier (tid) if this process was not created by
   pvm_spawn. pvm_mytid returns the tid of the calling process and can be
   called multiple times in an application.
2. *pvm_initsend()* The routine pvm_initsend clears the send buffer and prepares it
   for packing a new message.

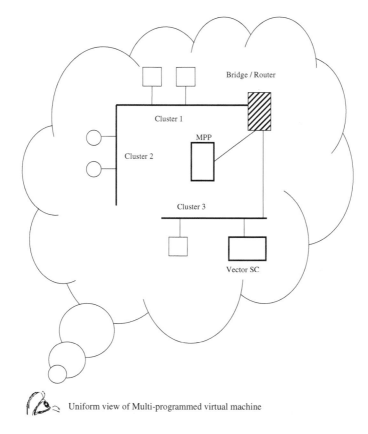

Uniform view of Multi-programmed virtual machine

Fig. 4.6 PVM Architectural Overview

3. *pvm_spwan( )* The routine pvm_spawn starts up n task copies of the executable named task. On systems that support environment, spawn passes selected variables in parent environment to children tasks.
4. *pvm_pkdouble( ), pvm_pkint( )* Each of the pvm_pk* routines packs an array of the given data type into the active send buffer.
5. *pvm_mcast( )* The routine pvm_mcast multicasts a message stored in the active send buffer to tasks specified in the array.
6. *pvm_send( )* The routine pvm_send sends a message stored in the active send buffer to the PVM process identified by tid.
7. *pvm_upkint( )* The pvm_upkint routine unpacks an array of the given data type from the active receive buffer.
8. *pvm_parent( )* The routine pvm_parent returns the tid of the process that spawned the calling process.
9. *pvm_recv( )* The routine pvm_recv blocks the process until a message with label message tag (msgtag) has arrived from tid. pvm_recv then places the message in a new active receive buffer, which also clears the current receive buffer.

10. *pvm_joingroup()* The routine pvm_ joingroup enrolls the calling task in the group and returns the instance number (inum) of this task in this group.
11. *pvm_barrier()* The routine pvm_barrier blocks the calling process until count members of the group have called pvm_barrier. The logical function of the pvm_barrier call is to provide a group synchronization. Once a given barrier has been successfully passed, the same group using the same group name can call pvm_barrier again.

4.2.5.1 Master PVM Algorithm

//Assume that the image is available in all the slaves

1. Divide the image into k triangles, where k is an integer greater than one.
2. Master processor will allocate the triangles to the slave processors.
3. //To send quality factor

   pvm_initsend(PvmDataDefault);
   pvm_pkdouble(&eps,k,tag); //eps is quality factor
   pvm_mcast(child, k, tag); // child is an array used to store tid of the slaves

4. //To send the triangle vertices

   for(i = 0; i < k; i ++)
   {
   pvm_initsend(PvmDataDefault);
   pvm_pkint((int*)(&tring[i]), 6, 1); //tring is a structure to store vertices the triangle
   pvm_send(child[i],tag);
   }

5. //To receive the compressed image size from the slaves
   for(i = 0; i < k; i ++)
   {
   pvm_recv(child[i],tag);
   pvm_upkint(size + i,1,1);
   }

6. // To recive the compressed image from slaves

   for(i = 0; i < k; i ++)
   {
   pvm_recv(child[i],tag);
   pvm_upkint((int*)(retbuf[i],9*size[i],1);
   }
   Write the compressed image in output file.

7. Write the compressed image in output file.

4.2.5.2 Slave PVM Algorithm

1. pvm_joingroup("slave");
2. //To receive quality factor

   pvm_recv(tid,tag);
   pvm_upkdouble(&eps,1,1);

3. // To receive vertices of the triangles

   pvm_recv(tid,tag);
   pvm_upkint((int*)(&tring),6,1);

4. pvm_barrier("slave",k);
5. Run BTTC sequential algorithm on allocated triangles by the master.
6. // To send size of the compressed image

   pvm_initsend(PvmDataDefault);
   pvm_pkint((int*)(&number,1,1);
   pvm_send(tid,tag);

7. // To send compressed image

   pvm_initsend(PvmDataDefault);
   pvm_pkint((int*)retbuf,number*9,1);
   pvm_send(tid,tag);

4.3 Experimental Results

To evaluate the performance of BTTC algorithm on PVM, several standard 8 bit test images were used. This section presents some results obtained on one such image—Lenna (512 × 512) shown in Fig. 4.7. Figure 4.8 shows the sample outcome of domain partition of this test image. The visual results of the algorithm on Lenna compressed at different levels of quality are illustrated in Fig. 4.9. Figure 4.10 shows the variation in peak-signal-to-noise-ratio with increasing quality factor.

The PVM algorithm was coded in C and executed on Intel machines connected via a 100 Mbps LAN. From 4.10 it can be seen that the peak signal to noise ratio of BTTC is nearly equal to the JPEG at different compression ratios. Speedup of the parallel BTTC on PVM is acceptable with varying number of processors as shown in Fig. 4.11. Figure 4.12 shows the timing diagram of the algorithm using two and four processors. Master sends the quality factor (e) to all the slaves as indicated by event number 1 in the timing profile of Fig. 4.12. The event number 2 indicates that the slaves have got the vertices of the triangles. After sending the vertices of the triangles to the respective slaves, master waits for the result and thus enters the wait region. Event number 3 and

Fig. 4.7 Original lenna
image

Fig. 4.8 Domain
triangulation for lenna at
compression ratio 3.19 using
PVM

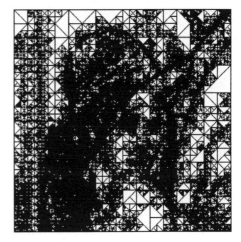

4 show that all the slaves have sent the size of the compressed image and
compressed image to the master. Once the master receives the messages from
all slaves, it creates the output file and exits the system. Figure 4.13 shows the
utilization diagram of BTTC algorithm on PVM for encoding lenna image on
four processors, using 12 slave tasks. Thus including the master program there
are $12 + 1 = 13$ tasks in total. The X-axis shows the time and Y-axis shows
the utilization of the 13 tasks.

The utilization graph can be roughly divided into two main regions. The
process encoding starts only after required data is passed to the respective slave
and each slave starts the work on its allotted task. This is shown in region 1
where most of the tasks are in computing stage. Region 2 starts when the
master receives its first message from slave when that particular task has

Fig. 4.9 Reconstructed image lenna at different compression ratios from *top left*: 2.46, 2.79, 3.19, and 3.91 using PVM

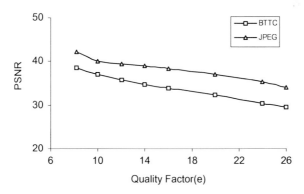

Fig. 4.10 Variation in Peak-Signal-to-Noise-ratio

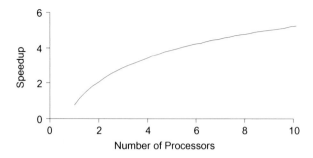

Fig. 4.11 Variation in speed up for the image lenna using PVM

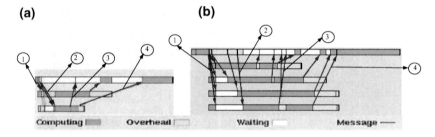

Fig. 4.12 Timing diagram of the BTTC algorithm on PVM algorithm using (**a**) two processors (**b**) four processors for the image lenna 512 × 512

■ The processor is performing the computation assigned to it.

■ This is the waiting state, where task is either waiting to send or receive a message from another task, which may be the master or slave.

■ Overhead involved in executing the PVM internal routines and functions. During this time the task does no work for the user, this time is used for synchronization, packing data, sending and receiving messages etc. These functions are internal to PVM

completed its job. Such tasks send their results to the master and exit PVM. We notice that number of tasks are reducing in region 2 and ultimately reduce to zero by the end of it. At the end of region 2, all the slaves have returned their data. The master after assembling the data and writing into the output file also departs from the PVM.

Fig. 4.13 Utilization
diagram of BTTC algorithm
on PVM using four
processors for the image
lenna 512 × 512

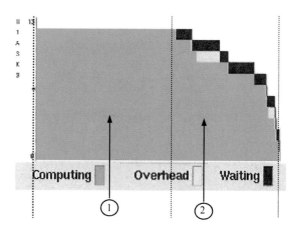

Table 4.1 Time complexities
and communications steps for
sequential and parallel BTTC
algorithms

Model	Time complexity for encoding	Communication steps
Sequential	$O(n \, log \, n)$	Nil
PRAM	$O\left(\frac{n}{p} log\left(\frac{n}{p}\right)\right)$	Nil
Hypercube	$O\left(\frac{n}{p}\left(log\left(\frac{n}{p}\right) + log \, p\right)\right)$ (or) $O\left(\frac{n}{p}\left(log\left(\frac{n}{p}\right) + k\right)\right)$	$O\left(\frac{n}{p} log \, p\right)$
2D Mesh	$O\left(\frac{n}{p}\left(log\left(\frac{n}{p}\right) + log \sqrt{p}\right)\right)$	$O\left(\frac{n}{p} log \sqrt{p}\right)$
Sparse mesh	$O\left(\frac{n}{p}\left(log\left(\frac{n}{p}\right) + log p\right)\right)$	$O\left(\frac{n}{p} log \, p\right)$

4.4 Conclusions

Image data compression is concerned with minimization of the number of information carrying units used to represent an image. In the Internet age, requirements
of image transmission are increasing steadily. In most cases, transmission of
acceptable quality images is infeasible without compression. Due to large memory
and/or transmission time demands of real images, it is desirable to consider parallel image compression. To speed up the image compression process we have
discussed four models for parallel implementation of BTTC image compression
algorithm. The time complexities and communication requirements are summarized in Table 4.1 for sequential as well as parallel BTTC algorithms. For all test
images, BTTC on PVM gives good speedup with increasing number of processors.

References

1. http://www.nas.nasa.gov/pubs/techsum/9495/final31398.html
2. Stauffer LM (1997) Dictionary compression on PRAM. Parallel Process Lett 7(3):297–308
3. http://www.npac.syr/edu/education/pub/demos/paralleljpeg.html
4. Jacson Dj, Mohmoud W (1996) Parallel pipelined fractal image compression using quadtree decomposition. Comput J 39(1):1–13
5. Jiang W, Bruton L (1998) Lossless color image compression using chromatic correlation. In: IEEE proceedings of data compression conference
6. Patterson DA, Hennessy JL (1990) Computer architecture: a quantitative approach. Morgan Kaufman Publishers, San Mateo
7. Cook GW, Delp J (1994) An investigation of JPEG image and video compression using parallel processing. In: Proceedings Of ICASSP, pp 437–440
8. Cook GW, Delp DJ (1996) An investigation of scalable SIMD I/O techniques with application to parallel JPEG compression. J Parallel Distrib Comput 53:111–128
9. Sibeyn JF (2000) Solving fundamental problems on sparse-meshes. IEEE Trans Parallel Distrib Sys 11(12):1324–1332
10. Shen K, Cook GW, Jamieson LH, Delp EJ (1994) An overview of parallel processing approach to image and video compression. In: Proceedings of SPIE, pp 197–208
11. Lee SS, Tanaka HT (2000) Parallel image segmentation with adaptive mesh. In: Proceedings of the international conference on pattern recognition (ICPR), pp 1635–1639
12. Lee S, Omachiand S, Aso H (2000) A parallel architecture for quadtree based fractal image compression. In: Proceedings of international conference on parallel processing (ICPP), pp 15–24
13. Jacson DJ, Blom T (1995) A parallel fractal image compression algorithm for hypercube multiprocessors. In: Proceedings of 27th southeastern symposium on system theory, pp 274–278
14. Miguet S, Pierson JM (2000) Quality and complexity bounds of load balancing algorithms for parallel image processing. Int J Pattern Recognit Artif Intell 14(4):463–476
15. Selim G. Akl (1989) The design and analysis of parallel algorithms. Prentice Hall Inc, Upper Saddle River, pp 26–98
16. http://www.netlib.org/pvm3/book/pvm-book.html
17. Miyahara M, Kotani K, Ralph Algazi V (1998) Objective picture quality scale (PQS) for image coding. IEEE Trans image process 46(5):1215–1225
18. Jackson DJ, Humphres CW (1997) A simple yet effective load balancing to the PVM software system. Parallel Comput 22:1647–1660
19. Agastino SD (2001) Parallelism and dictionary based data compression. Inf Sci 135:43–56
20. Giolmas N, Watson DW, Chelberg DM, Henstock PV, Yi JH, Siegel H (1999) Aspects of computational mode and data distribution for parallel range image segmentation. Parallel Comput 25:499–523
21. Redford J (2003) Parallelizing JPEG, In: SPC Proceedings, Dallas, 21 March–3 April 2003
22. Lee SS, Tanaka HT (2000) Parallel image segmentation with adaptive mesh. In: Proceedings of the international conference on pattern recognition (ICPR), pp 1635–1639
23. Lee S, Omachiand S, Aso H (2000) A parallel architecture for quadtree based fractal image compression. In: Proceedings of international conference on parallel processing (ICPP), pp 15–24
24. Prasad MVNK, Mishra VN, Shukla KK (2002) Implementation of BTTC image compression algorithm on parallel virtual machine. J Comput Soc India 32(3):1–8, ISSN 0254-7813
25. Akl SG (1989) The design and analysis of parallel algorithms. Prentice Hall Inc., Englewood Cliffs, pp 26–98
26. Prasad MVNK, Mishra VN, Shukla KK (2002) Implementation of BTTC image compression algorithm on parallel virtual machine (PVM). J Comput Soc India 32(3):31–38

Chapter 5
Conclusions and Future Directions

Abstract This Chapter gives overall concluding remarks discusses future research directions.

Keywords Triangulation · Performance evaluation · PSNR · PRAM · CREW

5.1 Concluding Remarks

A general survey of image compression algorithms has been presented in Chap. 1. Chapter 2 presented four new image compression algorithms: (1) Three triangle decomposition scheme, (2) Six triangle decomposition scheme, (3) Nine triangle decomposition scheme and (4) Delaunay triangulation scheme. Performance evaluation results of these algorithms using several standard 8 bit test images like lisaw, lenna, baboon etc. has been given. The nine triangle algorithm gave consistently better performance on all test images used.

The PSNR of nine triangle method is almost equal to binary tree triangular coding (BTTC) and is slightly less than JPEG. Visually, the quality of reconstructed image using nine triangle coding is as good as JPEG. Tests have been repeated on various images from different application domains like medical images, satellite remote sensing images and industrial images—on all these test images similar conclusions can be drawn.

The asymptotic time complexity of three, six, and nine triangle decomposition algorithms is the same, O($nlogn$) for coding and $\theta(n)$ for decoding. The quality achieved is acceptable for the three triangle algorithm and the six triangle algorithm and is very good for nine triangle algorithm. Delaunay triangulation algorithm has the property that it maximizes the minimum internal angle. The time complexity of the Delaunay triangulation algorithm is O(n^2logn) for coding and

Table 5.1 Summary of time complexities and communications steps for sequential and parallel domain decomposition algorithms

Model	Time complexity for encoding	Communication steps
Sequential	$O(n \log n)$	Nil
PRAM	$O\left(\frac{n}{p} \log\left(\frac{n}{p}\right)\right)$	Nil
Hypercube	$O\left(\frac{n}{p}\left(\log\left(\frac{n}{p}\right) + \log p\right)\right)$ (or) $O\left(\frac{n}{p}\left(\log\left(\frac{n}{p}\right) + k\right)\right)$	$O\left(\frac{n}{p} \log p\right)$
2-D mesh	$O\left(\frac{n}{p}\left(\log\left(\frac{n}{p}\right) + \log\sqrt{p}\right)\right)$	$O\left(\frac{n}{p} \log\sqrt{p}\right)$
Sparse mesh	$O\left(\frac{n}{p}\left(\log\left(\frac{n}{p}\right) + \log p\right)\right)$	$O\left(\frac{n}{p} \log p\right)$

$O(nlogn)$ for decoding, where n is the number of pixels in the image. The quality of the reconstructed image using Delaunay triangulation is slightly less than the BTTC image compression algorithm.

Domain decomposition algorithms using quality measures (AD, H, NMSE) and fuzzy geometry measure (FC) were presented in Chap. 3. AD as a basis for subdivision has the desirable properties of uniqueness and simplicity. Every gray value in the triangular region contributes to the AD measure leading to better noise immunity. Entropy gives the self-information rate of the triangle. NMSE summarizes the information of the parent triangle. FC offers the advantages of reduced triangulation and better noise immunity. All the partitioning methods presented in this Chapter gave consistently better performance than the BTTC on all test images. The quality of the reconstructed image using all the partitioning techniques significantly improves when compared to BTTC at similar compression ratios for all standard test images. Fuzzy compactness gives better quality when compared to the other partitioning methods.

Computing time for AD, Entropy, NMSE, and FC are high when compared to BTTC. All the partitioning methods proposed using quality measures execute in $O(nlogn)$ time for encoding and $\theta(n)$ time for decoding, where n is the number of pixels in the image. The BTTC algorithm and its variants are faster than the standard techniques—JPEG and JPEG2000.

Parallel Domain Decomposition algorithm on different architectures: (1) Concurrent Read Exclusive Write (CREW) Parallel Random Access Machine (PRAM), (2) Hyper cube, (3) 2-D Mesh, and (4) Sparse mesh were presented in Chap. 4. Time complexity of image encoding on all architectures has been discussed. The time complexities and communication steps are summarized in Table 5.1 for sequential as well as parallel algorithms.

Implementation of the domain decomposition algorithms on parallel virtual machine (PVM) environment using Master–Slave paradigm has been described. Algorithm gave acceptable speedup with increasing number of processors.

5.2 Future Directions

Image compression has become a major area of research due to the recent development and wide usage of multimedia applications. This book has presented five domain decomposition based image compression algorithms and evaluated their performance on sequential and parallel computers. Several interesting problems can be explored in this area. One can consider various quality measures in Delaunay compression algorithm instead of variance for placing the new vertex of the triangle at the barycenter of the triangle. Extension of all the proposed algorithms to 3D surface reconstruction problem and color images could be another fruitful research area. Implementation of Three, Six, Nine and Delaunay triangle compression algorithms on various parallel architectures and evaluation of their performance can be an interesting problem. The domain decomposition techniques discussed in the book can also be applied to morphing and other special effects.